MICHAEL WIESE PRODUCTIONS
www.mwp.com

We are delighted that you have found, and are enjoying, our books.

Since 1981, we've been all about providing filmmakers with the very best information on the craft of filmmaking: from screenwriting to funding, from directing to camera, acting, editing, distribution, and new media.

It is our goal to inspire and empower a generation (or two) of film and videomakers like yourself. But we want to go beyond providing you with just the basics. We want to shake you, and inspire you to reach for your dreams and go beyond what's been done before. Most films that come out each year waste our time and enslave our imaginations. We want to give you the confidence to create from your authentic center, to bring something from your own experience that will truly inspire others and bring humanity to its full potential — avoiding those urges to manufacture derivative work in order to be accepted.

Movies, television, the Internet, and new media all have incredible power to transform. As you prepare your next project, know that it is in your hands to choose to create something magnificent and enduring for generations to come.

This is not an impossible goal because you've got a little help. Our authors are some of the most creative mentors in the business, willing to share their hard-earned insights with you. Their books will point you in the right direction but, ultimately, it's up to you to seek that authentic something on which to spend your precious time.

We applaud your efforts and are here to support you. Let us hear from you.

Sincerely,

Michael Wiese
Filmmaker, Publisher

"*Digital Cinema: the Hollywood Insider's Guide to the Evolution of Storytelling* is a fantastic resource for filmmakers in the digital age. It not only comprehensively breaks down how digital video is changing the course of cinema forever, but also gives a firsthand account from the producers responsible for the digital revolution. This book serves as a manual for independent filmmakers seeking to understand the imminent metamorphosis of the industry in the digital age."

— Joana Vicente, Producer, Co-Founder
and Co-President of Blow Up Pictures

"*Digital Cinema* is funny, informative, and inspiring. Told with a lot of 'tough love,' it sorts out the confusing and frustrating world of trying to get a low budget movie made."

— Nicole Holofcener, Writer and Director
of *Lovely and Amazing*

"An invaluable guide for every writer who ever wanted to learn more about the business of Entertainment. Hsu and Taylor not only inform, but implore writers to understand the business they want to write for."

— Jon Katzman
Independent Producer/Television Executive

"Hsu and Taylor have hit their mark with *Digital Cinema*. Lots of great technical and creative information delivered with flair and humor. A strong recommend for both novices and experienced pros alike. Solid through and through."

— Mark J. Foley
Editor, *Videography Magazine*

DIGITAL
CINEMA

THE HOLLYWOOD INSIDER'S GUIDE
TO THE EVOLUTION OF STORYTELLING

THOM TAYLOR & MELINDA HSU

Published by Michael Wiese Productions
11288 Ventura Blvd., Suite 621
Studio City, CA 91604
tel. (818) 379-8799
fax (818) 986-3408
mw@mwp.com
www.mwp.com

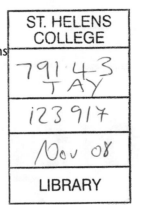

Cover Design: AG Design Company
Book Layout: Gina Mansfield
Editor: Arthur G. Insana

Printed by McNaughton & Gunn, Inc., Saline, Michigan
Manufactured in the United States of America

© 2003 Thom Taylor and Melinda Hsu

Library of Congress Cataloging-in-Publication Data

Taylor, Thom.
  Digital cinema : the Hollywood insiders guide to the evolution of storytelling / Thom Taylor & Melinda Hsu.
        p. cm.
Filmography: p.
  ISBN 0-941188-81-7
  1. Motion pictures--Production and direction. 2. Motion picture authorship. 3. Motion pictures--Marketing. 4. Digital video. I. Hsu, Melinda. II. Title.
  PN1995.9.P7T33 2003
  791.43--dc21

                              2003014458

To Martha & Yu Kao

>>> ACKNOWLEDGMENTS

To the reader, for thinking on the cutting edge and having the guts to make movies and tell stories on your own.

To Noah Lukeman, who believed in us (and this book) from the start, and without whose dogged pursuit and practical insights this book would have never reached its market. To Ken Lee and Michael Wiese, for their guidance and encouragement.

To Sara Lichterman, Mark Greenberg, James Tocher, Jeff Shapiro, Peter Dekom, Jon Feltheimer, Tom Ortenberg, Jennifer Champagne, Todd Perry, Scott Kroopf, Rich Martini, Kirby Kirsh, John Gallagher, and the many, many others who have been so helpful in the interview process.

To James Pike and Dianna Christakos, Melinda's high school Drama and English teachers, as well as her first creative champions.

And to both our families, for putting up with Thom's announcement at our wedding that "there's something very exciting that you may not know about yet, because around this time next year, we're having a... book published."

Thom Taylor & Melinda Hsu

Van Gogh's Ear

By Richard Martini

"Should I shoot digital? Can we afford 35-millimeter? What's the release print going to look like? How do I sell my film if no one famous is in it?"

These are all questions filmmakers face in the new digital century. For the past 100 years, 35-millimeter has dictated the market, as well as become the chosen medium in which filmmakers could work. Other formats appeared: 16-millimeter, then 8-millimeter, and my personal exposure to film began with an 8-millimeter pixelated film that I made in high school about a nuclear war. Well, actually, it began by looking at naughty 8-millimeter loops that my friend Billy Meyer found in his parents' cabin in Wisconsin, but that's another story.

When I was in film school at USC, I made a film about the wheelchair races at the Special Olympics. My "super-8" camera featured a button that allowed "super slow-mo," and when the gun fired to start the races, I'd hit the button. The footage of these wheelchair bound kids struggling in super slow motion to cross a white line 50 yards away was incredibly compelling. Although only 10 minutes long, this silent 8-millimeter film managed to win the International Film Festival in Mexico City in 1980.

It was probably at this point I realized that the content of the film was more powerful than its delivery. I went to work for writer-director Robert Towne out of film school, and learned the importance of the written word. But, as Robert is fond of pointing out, one of the most powerful scenes in cinema is when a young Vito Corleone murders his enemies in *Godfather II*, then walks across rooftops to join his infant son where he tells him, "Your father loves you very much."

Sometimes, images outweigh any words. I forged my own career out of writing and, in some cases, also directing, lightweight comedies such as *Three For the Road, You Can't Hurry Love,* or *Limit Up.* I mention them because making a feature using studio money and 35-millimeter film teaches a filmmaker how difficult it is to tell personal stories, or to do anything out of the ordinary that isn't packaged, sold, and reviewed properly. Thank God for digital cinema.

It was a challenge from a friend of mine that got me into the digital film world. Former editor at *Variety* and feature writer for *USA Today* Bruce Haring was doing an article about making digital movies and asked me how much it would cost for a consumer to make a feature-length project. I said to him, "Find me a digital camera, and I'll let you know how much." So, armed with a borrowed Canon XL1, and a Sony VX 1000, I set about to make a movie for as little money as I could.

I contrived a story around a digital camera; called *Camera,* it tells the story of a DV camera that's stolen from a video store, and goes on an adventure around the world, all told from the POV of the lens. Whoever takes the lens cap off tells the story. I was influenced by news of a group of teens that stole a camera, and filmed themselves shooting paint balls at homeless people. The tape wound up in the hands of the police. As Homer Simpson would say, "Dohhh!"

Armed with my two cameras, using the more photogenic Sony as the "picture camera," I crafted a story using improv actors who had appeared in my previous features. The inspiring question was, "How have cameras invaded our daily lives?" A jealous husband buys the camera from a pawnshop to spy on his wife, who, he thinks, is having an affair; it turns out that she's having an affair with the guy who installs the camera. The camera films a suicide attempt of a guy standing on a rooftop getting ready to jump — I happened to witness this in Santa Monica one day, so I took out my camera and recorded the event. Thankfully, the guy didn't jump, so I used it in the film. The camera films a commercial, witnesses a wedding, goes sky-diving with

Angie Everhart and a championship sky-diving team, and even stalks model Carol Alt. Carol told me a story about a fan who had asked her to say something nice on his camera — after she smiled and waved to "his friends back home," he refused to let her go, and stalked her until she was in tears. So we recreated that event. But those who view the film are not sure whether I'm really stalking Carol or not. The camera also winds up on the Mir space station, because the Russians had to resort to pawnshops to get cheaper equipment.

Finally, I wind up with the camera, Rich Martini, film guy — and I go around and ask people to appear in my "no budget" movie. Everyone says no, but oddly, they're the same people we have already seen in the movie. At the end, I ask a friend what he thinks I should do with the camera, and he says, "Why not make a film about a camera?" The final image is that of me setting up the first shot of the movie, in the video store where the camera was stolen. It ends with me saying "And... action!"

I tell you this story, because (A) you'll probably never see the movie, and (B) it's an example of how any dolt, even me, can make a movie out of nothing. I did my editing on a Media 100 at a friend's post-pro-duction house, and the film ultimately cost me the price of digital tape, $300. I submitted it to the Dogme Web site — not because I had planned to make a Dogme project, but because I had inadvertently fol-lowed the Dogme rules of filmmaking: no lights, no make-up, utilizing available locations, not a genre picture, per se (the Dogme rules remind me of a Danish play: existential, darkly hilarious, and hard to follow). When I saw Thomas Vinterburg's Dogme #1 movie, *Celebration*, shot on a single-chip DV camera, I was reminded of my experience with the Special Olympics film; how content trumps deliv-ery, when it comes to telling a compelling story.

Camera — Dogme #15 — had its world premiere at the "Digital Talkies" Film Festival in India in 2000. They put me up in a four-star hotel; the price of the hotel room each night was more expensive than the movie. Instead of making a $30-60,000 35-millimeter print, I was able to project the mini-DV on the Barco projection system, and it does an amazing job of translating digital images onto the big screen. I had done tests on 35-millimeter, which look great, but this was something else altogether. Every shaky camera move and silly joke of mine was bigger than life, and despite my trepidation, the movie managed to get laughs and praise from the audience of 3000 attendees. It was a fitting end to my journey, which began with a simple question, "How hard is it to make a digital movie?"

As a result of the screening, I was hired to shoot a commercial for a tour company in India, and while shooting the commercial, shot a documentary about Tibetan Refugees (which is being used by Amnesty International as part of its information packet on Tibet). It features the Dalai Lama, the Oracle of Tibet and other Tibetan notaries, none of whom I would have met, had I not brought my trusty DV camera with me, just in case.

I am co-director of the DIY Film Festival in Los Angeles, which features films made in a "Do It Yourself" style — not financed by any film studio, but put together with passion and individual chutzpah. Winners include a filmmaker from USC who went on to win the Chrysler Million Dollar Film Festival last year, and a retired fireman, who after spending two weeks trying to dig his fellow firemen out of the WTC, picked up his video camera to document their stories. His powerful documentary embodies what DIY filmmakers can achieve; moved by an event, or a story, a filmmaker picks up his or her camera and crafts a work of art.

After all, when painters pick up their paintbrushes, it's not because they are thinking of how much money they will make when they're finished. Imagine if Van Gogh had been thinking about the amount of return he was going to get on his investment from his life's work — it would have driven him crazy. Okay, it did drive him crazy. But any filmmaker can pick up a camera and create something out of nothing — hopefully without losing his or her soul, or ear, in the process.

It was Jean Renoir who said, to paraphrase, "When the cost of film-making is as much as a pencil and a piece of paper, then we'll find great artists." Well, now is that time. So when you've finished reading this book, pick up your camera and get to work. You never know where it might take you.

Rich Martini
Director of *Camera (Dogme #15)*, *Three for the Road*, *You can't Hurry Love*, and *Limit Up*
Co-Director of the Do-It-Yourself Film Festival in Los Angeles

>>>*TABLE OF CONTENTS*

>>>*THE BACKSTORY OF THE DIGITAL REVOLUTION*

For Nat Moss, the deciding factor was the attitude of *Let's just do it. We can get this done.* He and his writing partners didn't have to wait several years for the stars to align and the circumstances to be exactly right. Their movie was getting made.

By now, the independent digital feature *Washington Heights* has been through every step of the long road from conception to photography to theatrical distribution. Flash back a few years: New York City – Day. Alfredo Rodriguez de Villa and Nat Moss meet in the film program at the Columbia University School of the Arts. Alfredo goes on to become a globetrotting Spanish-language commercial producer, and Moss continues screenwriting while working a day job in Manhattan at a prestigious magazine. Their creative efforts, as often happens in the real lives of everyday people, are sometimes forced to take a back seat to their needs to pay the bills and have a somewhat normal existence — Alfredo's job requires frequent travel and intense production schedules; Moss and his wife work full time while caring for their first baby.

Enter actor Manny Perez (a Dominican actor from the Labyrinth Theater, which also spawned talents like Paul Calderon and Philip Seymour Hoffman). Manny had starred in Alfredo's thesis film at Columbia University, and as a young Latino actor, Perez was getting tired of playing "Drug Dealer #4" in other people's projects. Perez has a friend who has about $20,000 to put toward helping Perez make a film to star in, and in response to this opportunity, Perez has written a rough first draft of a father-son cop drama. Alfredo agrees to come on board as the project's director, and he begins rewriting the script with Moss as co-writer.

Moss, Alfredo, and Perez then come up with a completely new treatment about an artist in a predominantly Dominican neighborhood of New York City who has to take over his dad's corner-store bodega when his dad gets shot. Because of the actors who agree to lend their names to the project as part of the package (such as Lauren Velez of *I Like It Like That*, who originally is going to play the love interest, but has to leave the project at the last minute — literally days before shooting begins — due to an injury), they have letters of intent to show production companies. All these people are being sold an idea, and people are jumping on board before they see the finished product. It's a testimony to the self-generating momentum that a project has once you begin to tell people that you're actually going to make a film and nothing is going to stop you.

Initially, they want to shoot the low-budget feature on film, either 16-millimeter or Super 16-millimeter (Mike Figgis' choice on *Leaving Las Vegas*). The decision to use digital video comes when the reality of the budget hits them. Tests at Swiss Effects, Duart, and Efilm convince Alfredo that the aesthetic line between film and DV is getting very subtle. Also, he's meeting very experienced cinematographers who advocate shooting digital video, including Claudio Chea, who has just shot *Piñero* using the Canon XL1 mini-DV camera. In addition, all this is happening while digitally shot films such as *Chuck and Buck* and *Series 7: The Contenders* are causing a small sensation at festivals and movie theaters. *Celebration* also serves as a role model in the sense that all of a sudden you can tell an amazing story, and make a very complex film, on video, with a very quick, nervous, handheld camera that can capture reality very quickly. With financing almost in place, Alfredo and his team prepare for the shoot. Their journey unfolds in the chapters to come.

What is the digital revolution, and what does it mean to the filmmaker, the media industry, and the movie-going audience? Will the increasing affordability and accessibility of digital video result in a flood of bad movies by amateurs? Or will it make "film" a much more dynamic and inclusive medium, actually raising the creative bar because there will be so many more people in the market competing with product? How do you go about making your own DV project, and what are the pros and cons versus film? Are celluloid film and film projection really going to go the way of the LP record (or even worse, the 8-track tape)?

This book is written for anybody who has a story to tell, and a desire to bring a script to life. It also is written for anybody else who works in the movie business or enjoys movies, and has a spark of curiosity about what has brought the digital revolution this far, and which forces will determine what happens next. We believe that digital tools have democratized the filmmaking process, but that they have not yet truly changed the Hollywood processes by which most movies get seen or make money. The promise of being able to craft, control, and create your own vision is real; that said, beware of "techno-lust" and blind belief in the hype of the media, the manufacturers, and the technology holders who tell you that they have all the answers.

To enter, embrace and have an edge in today's Hollywood — or to circumvent it entirely — you need to know what the new technology is, and what it's capable of doing. In charting the movie industry's journey to this turning point, we will demystify the production trenches, find out what the money people really think, take a good look at whether DV has film studios and distributors fearing that they'll be squeezed out of their dominant roles, and debate whether they ought to be scared. In the meantime, we will convey the hands-on experience of independent media artists, who in some cases are armed only with their dreams, their determination and their DV cameras, while they attempt to get their projects shot, edited, and seen in an increasingly crowded marketplace.

Why is *storytelling* exciting to people? Going back to our cave-dwelling ancestors sitting around the fire, the human impulse to entertain, provoke, move, enlighten, and share has shaped our whole history of dramatic, written, and visual work. There is a very basic human need for translating internal thoughts and emotions into a medium that can effectively and affectingly convey them to others, whether through song, theater, still photographs, celluloid film, or digital recordings. Looking at those parts of the human experience that are universal, digital technology promises a quantum leap in access to visual storytelling tools. Initially, that was a cause for some unease in the film industry, although the current mood contains as much backlash as it does acceptance towards digitally acquired images as a broadening of the filmmaker's palette, nothing more and nothing less.

Digital video cameras, digital production, digital post-production, digital projection — what's all the fuss? Nobody made apocalyptic industry-wide predictions when computers, screenwriting software, and how-to books gave everybody and her mother access to the tools and knowledge of a screenwriter's craft. There are a million scripts out there, and the fact that anyone can sit down and write one doesn't have anything to do with which ones are good, or, more to the point, ever get seen, let alone made into movies (of which only some, in turn, are ever seen or are good). The difference between screenwriting and digital cinema, though, is that John Q. Artist, thousand-dollar camera in hand, can run out into his Missouri hometown and shoot a hundred hours of footage to be edited on his home computer. Voila, he has a two-hour feature, for pennies compared to the cost of a film production, and with a technological flexibility and durability that threatens to make celluloid a thing of the past.

What's equally interesting is how many citizens there are with a story to tell. Not to say that every first-timer is going to have the craft or the resources to make a product to rival those of big Hollywood or independent names. But there is a very fundamental human need to share experiences, and to have some method of control and conveyance of what is important to us. If that weren't true, why would NASA scientists have made such a point of including carefully selected images on the surface of the Voyager spacecraft, in the hopes of finding an audience in outer space someday? The same goes for prehistoric cave drawings.

Those were the first picture shows, bonding cave-dweller audiences together because of someone's ability to externalize an internal experience and affect others with that externalization. Cave drawings and the Voyager spacecraft are both examples of the intersection of new technology (whether paint pigment or space travel) and the human desire to tell a story. The growth of digital video, and ongoing advances in the ways people can get their stories seen by audiences around the world, will satisfy and foster our storytelling needs like never before.

That's the good news, and we will get into some of the downsides of the populist model later. But first, to appreciate the context of the DV debate and the evolution of the craft, consider the astonishing emergence of digital cinema from 1998 to the present:

> *Celebration* convinced audiences and critics in 1998 that a feature shot on digital video could be compelling, entertaining, and powerful. Although some viewers had trouble adjusting to the intentionally grainy, hand-held quality of the image, the digital feature's reliance on available light sources and minimalist settings allowed the characters' conflicts to take center stage. The movie also increased the buzz surrounding Dogme (or Dogma) 95's "Vow of Chastity," which challenged filmmakers to abandon mainstream (i.e. Hollywood) conventions of artificial lighting, fake sets and props, soundtracks, visual effects, unrealistic premises, and even directors' credits. Although most directors who have been inspired by Dogme 95 still put their names on their projects, and although the Vow of Chastity actually calls for the use of 35-millimeter film, DV storytellers often refer to a Dogme-esque search for the truth in their characters and conflicts — a search that they claim is easier and more effective in the digital medium.

> Computer editing software, pioneered by professional Avid editors, went on the market for the average consumer. Final Cut Pro for the Macintosh was joined by a variety of Mac- and PC-compatible competitors such as Adobe Premiere,

iMovie and Media Tools. Together with cheaper digital video cameras, visual effects software, and music composing software, the pieces of a home movie studio became increasingly available to independent and first-time filmmakers.

> An Internet-driven word-of-mouth phenomenon helped *The Blair Witch Project* gross over $300 million worldwide in 1999 after being made for virtually nothing. Although not shot solely on digital video, the film's multiple-format approach created the first widespread public awareness of the DV medium and its (enormous) profit potential.

> An exponential increase in digital movies from 1999 to the present brought audiences *Buena Vista Social Club* directed by Wim Wenders, *Time Code* directed by Mike Figgis, *Bamboozled* directed by Spike Lee, *Dancer In The Dark* directed by Lars von Trier, *The Anniversary Party* co-directed by Jennifer Jason Leigh and Alan Cumming, *28 Days Later* directed by Danny Boyle, and *Full Frontal* directed by Steven Soderbergh, just to name a few.

> Actors such as Ethan Hawke and Campbell Scott have turned to the DV medium to direct; other new directors are groomed by production companies such as Madstone, InDigEnt, and Blow Up Pictures to have their first shots at DV features, rather than wait longer to go the more expensive route of helming a celluloid film.

> Technological advances have accelerated to meet the market's demands, most notably the Cine Alta 24-P developed by Sony for George Lucas' use on *Episode II: Attack of the Clones*. The Cine Alta shoots 24 frames per second, just as a film camera would; compared to earlier DV cameras that shot on a video ratio of 30fps, the Cine Alta is able to produce an image almost identical to that of film. Granted, the Cine Alta is not cheap to rent, but its capabilities (for example, instant dailies that can be viewed on set and sent electronically to production and effects supervisors anywhere in the world) have convinced other studio productions to adopt it as their tool of choice.

> Internet exhibitors, digital video festivals, and self-distribution have all created opportunities for do-it-yourself DV filmmakers to reach audiences. While DV images still can't match the depth and contrast of film, technology such as Magic Bullet (developed by former Industrial Light & Magic whizzes) can now help eradicate the differences in visual quality. Regardless, for budget, logistical, and creative reasons, DV is rapidly overtaking other formats for new filmmakers seeking to make their marks. By the year 2001, the Sundance Festival accepted 23 digital features and projected 18 digitally.

> Digital pipelines are becoming increasingly important in postproduction, particularly when rushed schedules crunch the turnaround times required among special effects teams, physical production, and studio executives. With more and more projects shot digitally, and many acquired-on-film features going through post-production in the form of a digital intermediate, the transition to digital projection may be inevitable. Digital champions laud the viewing quality and cost savings possible through new technology that would eliminate the need for printing and shipping degradable celluloid. To others, especially the theaters and studios who look to each other to absorb the cost of retrofitting more than 30,000 existing projection facilities, an all-digital future remains a distant hypothetical. But digital television, faster Internet streaming and downloading capabilities, and digital projection innovations are on the rise. Even celluloid-based mainstays such as Technicolor are exploring how to transition into a future where worldwide audiences will line up for movies sent to their theaters electronically via satellite and then projected digitally and perfectly, with every image exactly as the filmmakers intended it to be seen. (We know DV isn't "film," but, in fact, DV isn't video, either, because there's no video signal — it's ones and zeroes. So we will use the honored nomenclature of "filmmaker" to refer to the broad pool of cinema artists — again, those with visual stories to tell, digitally or otherwise.)

If the digital era is really upon us, with cheap, fast productions under the total control of the filmmaker, studios had better rethink the bloated budgets and years-long timetables of their projects in order to compete with the new, hungry, capable, and affordably equipped DV filmmaker. Or so the prediction goes. But the Hollywood machine remains forbiddingly complex and self-protective. It takes more than just the variable of being able to control and produce an individual vision for a change to be seen quickly, either in the industry establishment or in what is shown in theaters. Through profiling the current markets and their major players, we will examine the financiers, buyers, and audiences that determine how many DV films ever get purchased or seen. We will also get the uncensored perspectives of acquisitions representatives, distributors, agents, and producers who are deluged with finished and embryonic DV projects that may never see the light of day.

That said, DV filmmakers are still raving about how they can tell the stories they want for a fraction of the cost, with more time for actors and artistic integrity, with fewer constraints in the logistics of production and post-production. Taking one step back to what the realities of film production have been in the past, here's a comparison between shooting on film and shooting on DV. Say we want to shoot this scene:

```
INT.   COFFEE SHOP — DAY


Bright morning sunlight.  The finale of a lover's
quarrel.  Janice throws a glass of water in her
boyfriend's face.

                    JANICE
              You dog!
```

It may be no surprise that shooting this scene on color 16-millimeter film would be much more expensive than shooting it on digital video. But to see exactly why, let's look at the approximate costs of both, starting with the film option:

Film permit:	$1590 a day
On a low-budget film set, unavoidable expenses arise, because there is no way to hide a film crew, which means that the production needs to get a film permit. A location permit in, for example, the city of West Hollywood, California costs $200 a day for intermittent pedestrian control, $400 to have equipment on the street, $300 for the application fee, $450 for the processing fee, and $60 an hour for a deputy with a four-hour minimum, or $240. This brings the total cost of a one-day film permit to $1590 (to shoot on Sunset Boulevard, add $400 — not even including additional fire safety; for instance, a shoot in Beverly Hills requires a Fire Department representative to be on hand while you shoot. For bigger productions, you'll also pay Beverly Hills to have a Fire Department truck standing by on location, just in case, and you'll need to budget at least $600 for the Fire Department's involvement).	
Location rental:	**$ 500 a day**
It's not unusual for locations to charge fees that include electricity usage, compensation for the time of a staff member to be on hand during filming, and an hourly rental. Assuming that the film crew needs a modest five hours to load in equipment, pre-light the set, shoot the scenes, and load out equipment, to shoot Janice's scene in an urban location this fee may be in the range of $500.	Total of $2090 each day

Camera rental:	$2000 a day
Renting 16-millimeter camera package (including lenses, camera, battery pack, tripod, other accessories, and insurance).	Total of $4090 each day
Lighting and grip rental:	**$1500 a day**
Lighting and grip equipment, plus a small rental truck to transport all the equipment: $1500 a day, plus parking fees and insurance.	Total of $5590 each day
Film stock:	**$ 300 a day**
One 400-foot roll of color 16-millimeter film costs $130 and lasts about 10 minutes. If you're shooting a frugal six-to-one ratio, or six takes for every shot, you might go through two or three rolls of film per day, costing around $300 a day. This is just the price of the film stock itself, and does not include any developing, processing, or printing fees.	Total of $5890 each day
Craft services:	**$ 136 a day**
Snacks, drinks, and a person to set up and replenish the craft services table would typically cost $8 per head times 17 people on set = $136.	Total of $6026 each day
Meals:	**$255 a day**
A catered meal has to be served on set every six hours. If you are shooting with a union crew (which brings on a whole other level of expenses in exchange for the crew's expertise), serving the meal a few minutes late incurs hundreds of dollars in union penalties. Assuming that this is a non-union shoot with only one meal break, a caterer could bring in a simple, hot meal for $15 per head times 17 people = $255.	Total of $6281 each day

Minimum total of film shoot:	$6000 a day

Even if every crew member and actor is working for free (this would be unusual with a crew of any experience), a single shooting day on this non-union, low-budget 16-millimeter film set costs at least $6,000.

Other costs:

A non-guerrilla film production, for legal, ethical, and economic reasons, also requires equipment insurance policies, workers' compensation insurance, general liability insurance, and errors and omissions insurance (think another $5,000 – $10,000). A completion bond could add on an additional $25,000 (a completion bond is a form of insurance to guarantee investors that the film will end up in a finished form; in the event that the filmmaker becomes unable to finish production for any reason, the completion bond company literally takes possession of the film so that investors don't lose all their money). Post-production usually matches the in-the-can cost of shooting the film. In other words, if you spent $108,000 for an eighteen-day ($6,000 a day) feature film shoot, you might expect to spend another $100,000 to get your footage developed, edited, scored, sound-mixed, and printed out on film.

Then there's another kind of cost, which is time. Back to our film set:	
Equipment load-in and setup of lighting and camera:	1 to 2 hours at a minimum
Takes possible on a low-budget ratio:	4 to 7 takes
Time between takes:	5 to 15 minutes

This includes touching up makeup, checking to make sure the camera gate is clean, tweaking lights, giving actors notes on performance, resetting props, slating, etc. If the camera is moving to a new position, all lights and focus marks have to be adjusted, which eats up time, as well. If a shot calls for dolly track, expect a set-up and camera rehearsal of one to two hours.

What a single take on this set might look like:	5 to 15 minutes

Actor and actress sit in their places at the table while the director talks the scene through with them again. Makeup artist retouches actor's makeup, which had water thrown on it in the previous take. Boom operator maneuvers so that no shadows fall into frame. First assistant cameraman walks a tape measure from the camera to the actress's face, checking lens focus. Second assistant cameraman fills out a camera report noting the kind of film stock, length of lens, and types of filters for reference in lab processing later; he also gets a slate ready with the film roll number, shot name and take number.

Director of photography takes a reading with a light meter, asks the gaffer to take off a layer of diffusion paper from one of the lights. Gaffer does so; the DP takes another reading. A grip moves in with a bounce board, reflecting light up onto the actress's face so that her eyes don't look sunken. A production assistant helps stock the craft services table. Sound recordist checks microphone levels with actors. Art department assistant brings a fresh glass of water; continuity supervisor uses a Polaroid to see if the new water level matches the one from the establishing master shot; script supervisor makes sure that this shot will cut with the other shots in the scene.

Location manager shows a passerby a copy of the film permit. Director looks through the camera eyepiece to approve the frame. The cinematographer gets behind the camera, calls for a boom check. Boom operator makes sure the microphone is out of frame. Assistant director asks, "Sound ready? Camera ready?" and waits for go-aheads. The DP calls for "marker in," and the 2nd AC puts the slate into frame.

AD says, "Roll sound," and after the sound recordist confirms that they're recording, "Roll camera." DP starts rolling film and reports "Speed" when the film is running at the proper rate through the camera. 2nd AC calls out the shot name and take number, and either slaps the sticks shut (or hits the time code beep if the extra $50 a day is being spent to rent a time-coded slate) for later sync-up between picture and sound.

Director calls, "Action." Janice says her line and throws her water in her boyfriend's face.

This fifteen-person skeleton crew, plus the two actors, will need a hot meal every six hours, restroom facilities, private changing and holding areas for actors, and water, coffee, drinks, and substantial snacks for the duration of the shoot.

To shoot the same scene on DV using only available daylight, a director and actors could go in without a permit or location rental and be done before anyone realized what was happening, saving over $2000 right off the bat (we are not actually recommending that you go shoot without permits, but these are the facts).

Here's how the costs on the DV set compare:

DV camera:	**$1200 to $4000**
Owning a DV camera is a worthwhile investment if you're going to be shooting for more than a few days. On the other hand, it's not hard to get the use of one for free, either through your local public access TV station or through a trusting friend.	
DV tape stock:	**$10 a day**
One 60-minute DV tape costs about $10. Shooting more than sixty minutes of footage per day is certainly possible, but can prove unwieldy and expensive in the editing phase.	Total of $10 each day

Lavaliere microphone and radio receiver:	$75 a day
This is an optional rental, but it greatly improves sound quality and gives additional flexibility in sound editing later. This kind of small microphone, plus the radio receiver that attaches to the camera, can be rented for $75 a day.	Total of $85 each day
Craft services:	$40 a day
$40 will buy a lot of snacks for four people.	Total of $125 each day
Meals:	$60 a day
$60 will take the four of you to a very nice lunch. (Splurging for a hot, healthy, and appetizing meal will pay off in goodwill and patience from the cast and crew.)	Total of $185 each day
Minimum total of digital video shoot:	$185 a day

Assuming the camera is already owned or has been borrowed by the filmmaker and that everyone is working for free, food, microphone, and tape stock come to $185. Even factoring in the cost of a $2500 middle-of-the-road camera and accessories, at this daily rate an eighteen-day DV shoot would cost $5830, or less than one day on the film set.

Time is the other clear savings on the DV set. Specifically:

Time for complete setup:	10 to 15 minutes

This includes putting the lavaliere microphone on the actress.

Takes possible:	As many as will fit on a 60-minute tape

Time between takes:	0 to 5 minutes

The director can roll tape continuously while giving acting notes, checking continuity, and drying the actor's face and shirt.

What a single take on this set might look like:

DP holds DV camera in one hand, running tape continuously, and checks sound levels from Janice's lavaliere microphone while director talks the scene through again with the actor and actress. Director and cinematographer sit on chairs next to the two actors. At a glance, it looks like the four of them are having coffee together.

Director double-checks the cinematographer's frame and says "Action." Janice says her line and throws her water in her boyfriend's face.

Meals, restroom facilities, private changing, and holding areas for actors, and water, coffee, drinks, and snacks still apply, although the separate camera operator is optional, as is the lavaliere microphone.

In documentaries, the finished product can be helped even more by DV's advantages. Not least of which is the ability to hide the camera completely, since some documentary situations benefit from the camera being unnoticed, and some documentary subjects require it.

But the cheapness of the shoot doesn't eliminate the post-production costs. Euphoric reports of the ease and speed of DV shooting rarely elaborate on the editing process, where dozens of hours of footage need computer memory storage space as well as real-time importing from the DV tape to the computer drive, often in five-minute chunks to safeguard against glitches. Logging and transferring footage onto self-owned or rented hard drives is extremely time-consuming and sometimes very expensive. The organization required increases in pro-portion to the amount of footage shot, especially since, in the interests of conserving computer memory, a filmmaker may have to pick and choose only a few takes to import and edit from, while still keeping the other existing takes on tape for later review and possible use.

Given the enormous logistical undertaking of editing a DV feature with copious raw footage, it can be well worth the money to hire a professional editor who offers expertise, perspective, an editing studio, and hard drive space. Weekly rates for such editors start in the range of $2000, and it's not uncommon for a feature film to need at least eight weeks in the editing room. Even a home editing software package will cost $1000, assuming the filmmaker already has a computer with the speed and memory to be effective. Add the fees for outputting to a digital beta sub-master tape, sound sweetening, transferring to a film negative, and striking even one print, and the made-for-nothing DV feature can suddenly cost over $50,000 (of course, there's always the hope that your story and approach will garner enough attention in its raw video form to get someone else to put up the money for the post).

The other major sacrifice in shooting on DV is the look of film, which technically means depth, grain, dynamic color range, and contrast, although transfer processes are getting better and better and less and less expensive (keep in mind that "less expensive" currently means DV-to-film transfer fees of $180 per minute, or $18,000 for a 100-minute feature, as opposed to much higher costs just a few years ago), and digital projection presents an entirely different category of viewing quality and durability. As importantly, however, some who are gun shy of DV fear a perceived loss of credibility and marketability in the film community, where, if no one wants to buy your product, it remains just as unseen a vision as if you'd never had the tools to make it in the first place.

To some extent, distributors control whose vision is seen, since they are the ones who purchase films and get them shown to the rest of the world. And on that side of the business, there is much more wariness concerning the new deluge of digital product. DV has unquestionably increased the number of competitors in the pool of completed features looking for distribution, and many would argue that DV's accessibility has also lowered the average quality of the products. No matter what kind of camera was used to shoot a movie, though, a film's appeal to distributors relies heavily on elements such as recognizable "name" actors in the lead roles (especially when trying to market a U.S. film to audiences in other countries) and the universality of the film's subject (for instance, baseball movies have typically not done well in non-U.S. territories).

Distributors have to be willing to stake their own resources and credibility on a film before they'll commit money to wooing today's fickle audiences, who have more and more sources of entertainment to choose from. Compelling stories and characters, distributors say, are what they require, though it seems that having a pretty girl take her shirt off will do almost as well. At any rate, the question is whether the DV medium serves the goals of distributors seeking maximum audience appeal. On the pro side, some acquisitions representatives feel that DV allows a vigorous and intimate creative approach; for others, however, the look of the DV image is an aesthetic and marketing turn-off. Whatever their perspectives on digital video, distributors are hard to reach and even harder to impress. For this reason, some independent filmmakers self-distribute their DV features, and we'll follow the steps of that journey, as well.

In DV research and development, Sony, Microsoft, and other high-tech companies are anxious not to be left behind in offering cutting-edge products for all phases of production, post, and distribution. But when it comes to the logical next step of digital projection, studio giants are reluctant to pick up the multi-billion dollar tab to convert theaters. Theater owners who don't want to pay to fix something that, in their opinion, isn't broke are not anxious to step forward either. Partly as a result of limited digital projection facilities for digitally shot films, DV is still being transferred to celluloid and is often still seen as a step down in aesthetics and legitimacy. In other words, it's constantly getting easier to make movies, but just as hard or even harder to get them seen in optimal conditions, acquired by distributors, and shown to widespread audiences. Festivals and Internet venues encourage digital video submissions and authorship, but competition increases in direct proportion to the opportunities presented.

Still, many companies are giving evidence of their intentions to pioneer, develop, and fund digital product. Artisan (the folks who brought you *The Blair Witch Project*) has made efforts to produce slates of digital features; Blow Up Pictures, InDigEnt, Madstone, and numerous other producers are in an accelerating competition to capture DV audiences. A groundswell of support for DV is also making itself clear in the international film community and even in major Hollywood studios, with potential return on investment motivating those who may be aesthetically neutral regarding DV versus celluloid.

THE WRAP

> From *Celebration* to *Star Wars Episode II: Attack of the Clones*, digital image acquisition and technological advances are continuing to establish critical and commercial viability for non-celluloid projects. Whether this results in better movies is still dependent on the strength of the story and the craft involved in telling it.

> Digital image acquisition has not changed the way the movie industry works, yet. Distributors still control whether the majority of features get seen in theaters, and exhibitors are still gun-shy of undertaking a costly and arguably premature conversion to digital projection.

> Celluloid isn't dead. But the best empowerment for filmmakers is to be aware of the evolving capabilities of digital image acquisition and post-production without being either overly rosy or needlessly close-minded about what digital promises for individual expression.

To smaller production and distribution companies, digital movies offer creative liberty, as well as make economic sense. These newer companies look to build clout from controlling their product, identifying the unmet needs of the market, and strengthening relationships with established members of the industry. DV offers inroads to all these strategic fronts, and business developers don't have to search far for confirmation that DV is here to stay. George Lucas shot *Episode II: Attack of the Clones* primarily on digital and is pushing for widespread digital projection as soon as possible. He claims that digital projection is aesthetically better, and also truer to the director's vision, than traditional celluloid is, and sees both digital filmmaking and digital projection as the inevitable standard of the future.

So, if you think George Lucas has no idea what he's talking about, put this book down. Otherwise, read on.

PART I
MAKING
IT HAPPEN

chapter
two

>>>*WRITINGS ON THE WALL*

Storytelling is one of the oldest human impulses. Prehistoric cave drawings and the tradition of gathering around the fire satisfied the same need that digital video does today: allowing individuals to share their visions with others in order to entertain, illuminate, and inspire them. When digital video first appeared on the filmmaking scene, it was heralded as a revolution that would quickly render film (and traditional Hollywood) obsolete. Those predictions proved premature for both technical and aesthetic reasons, but change has begun, and is underway. In this chapter, we hear from filmmakers on both sides of the digital divide: those who say that it's the best opportunity for new voices to share their visions with audiences, and those who caution that the limitations of DV are more severe than first meet the eye. And unfortunately for the filmmaker on a tight budget, these limitations are especially punishing in standard-definition digital video (i.e. images from even a high-end "prosumer" mini-DV camera), as opposed to high-definition or HD digital video.

In debating the aesthetic and intrinsic value of digital video, there are three main issues to haunt the young filmmaker at night: *freedom*, *legitimacy*, and *look*.

FREEDOM
If you use digital not for cost-cutting but for creative reasons, then it can be a powerful storytelling and aesthetic choice. One digital movie that comes to mind is *Tape*, which could not have been shot with conventional film cameras and lighting setups, because it all takes place in a small hotel room. Director Richard Linklater used the DV format to push for innovations in camera angles and creative storytelling in this adaptation of a stage play about three twenty-something friends who

confront each other about a rape that happened in high school. In successful uses of digital video formats, often the filmmaker has explored the questions of what you can do with digital image acquisition that you can*not* do conventionally.

Furthermore, some choose to make digital origination abundantly clear as part of the storytelling. In *Full Frontal*, director Steven Soderbergh gave a voyeuristic realism to his narrative by shooting most of the feature in raw-looking, handheld digital video. This, in contrast to the gorgeous perfection of the 35-millimeter footage of the movie-within-the-movie starring Julia Roberts and Blair Underwood, gave the audience different contexts for viewing, evaluating, and responding to the lives within both movies. Sometimes you can make a strong creative choice for something that doesn't exactly resemble either film or video: a new kind of look with its own beauty, embracing the differences rather than trying to disguise them.

Choices in format become critical here — do you use very affordable mini-DV with lower image resolution but greater mobility, or do you go for a high-definition but much more expensive 24fps digital format? Eva Kolodner, vice-president for development and production at Madstone Films, says the company chose to shoot 24P HD on *Rhinoceros Eyes* because it's set in a prop house that's full of rich, beautiful detail, and the story is all about art. In contrast, mini-DV's strengths — kinetic motion, intimacy with actors, and being able to work in small spaces — would have been a shortcoming for the project. The wide spectrum of digital video formats gives you the opportunity to shape the viewer response with the chosen visual medium as much as with camera angles and actors' directions, plot twists, production design, and all the other facets that make up a piece as a whole.

Digital may also give you the physical ability to get places you couldn't get with a truckful of film equipment and accompanying crewmembers. Juan de la Torre is a documentary filmmaker and producer for National Geographic and the Discovery Channel who took a lightweight camera and lenses on his treks into Guatemala and Costa Rica to shoot digital video for a documentary series. This is vastly preferable to what this kind of wildlife shooting used to be like, where a crew might be camped out in the jungle for days, and then run out of film at the moment of truth. "We used a Canon XL1, and you can do pretty cool stuff, even at night," de la Torre said. "On the Costa Rica shoot, I was working with crocodiles, and we were a two-day horse ride into the jungle with the cameras in our backpacks. It was pretty rugged — raining, steamy, chickens dying." (The chickens were to be used as bait for lassoing crocodiles.) "And the cameras just worked. It's cheaper and more effective than film, and you are not as encumbered. If you're a filmmaker working in a rough environment, even a guerrilla filmmaker in an urban environment, digital is great."

De la Torre is getting ready to shoot a feature film as well, and will probably go with digital video instead of film. He's found, as many filmmakers have, that if you really want your story to be told, you can't always be a purist, and you have to go with what's economically viable. That's the compromise that many filmmakers have to face — sacrifice the film image for getting the story out there. However, the beauty of DV is that for $10,000 you can own your own studio.

That kind of freedom fosters its own aesthetic, and there's a lot to be said for not having to get permission to make your movie the way you want to. And in addition to independence in shooting and finishing a film on your own, you may have fewer lighting requirements, if you want a raw, gritty look; DV sensitivity to light aside, though, it's usually going to be worth your while to spend the money and hire or have the expertise to light a digital video shoot with just as much depth and care as you would a film shoot. But it's agreed that the smaller size of the camera and crew allows for an intimacy among actors and directors, because the camera and the technology behind acquiring the image become much more invisible than they would on a film shoot. Part of that is because setups and multiple takes can happen so quickly; often, filmmakers are able to exploit this advantage in also staying in the moment with the story's plot and the characters' emotions. Finally, post-production manipulation becomes much easier for projects that originated on digital, even if you're using a Mac G4 and a bootlegged copy of AfterEffects in your living room, not that we condone bootlegging.

Additionally, shooting on digital may facilitate your communication with an audience by electronic means. For example, the *Texas Legacy* project is a digital documentary intended for grassroots distribution on the Internet. Through an ongoing compilation of interviews taken from a wide cross-section of Texas society, the documentary offers insights into the history, change, and future of Texas at the level of the individual, the community, and the state as a whole. Eventually, streaming video will allow audience members to access the interviews and do research through an online database. This kind of interactive viewing experience not only serves a practical purpose in outreach and education, but also completes the intended aesthetic of creating a vibrant, dynamic experience for the audience, as well as the documentary's subjects.[1]

Notice that *cheaper* is not a guaranteed advantage of going the digital route. Post-production typically costs at least as much as what you paid just to get the movie shot. Making a movie, even on a micro-shoestring, always costs much more than you expect. It's kind of like planning a wedding. There's always someone else who shows up needing food, lodging, and clothes; and always a vendor who charges five times what you were expecting. And the same kind of momentum can possess you: *well, we want to do this right, we've come this far, we can't stop now, let's just put those extra five things on a credit card.*

But we're not criticizing the desire to finish a feature project and do it in the way that seems best to you. This impulse comes out of the human need to share stories, and there were doubtless some cavemen and cavewomen back in the day who had to borrow pigment and charcoal from friends in order to get the rest of that painting up on the

---

[1] "From DV to PC," David Weisman, *IDA Journal*, October 2002

cave wall. So, one way or another, people use the medium's freedoms to their advantage, and all these digital movies get made through inspiration, drive, and opportunity, and then the market gets flooded with product. This adds a new challenge in terms of getting your material seen, but it's all part of the transitional time we're in.

What's exciting is that digital gives people an opportunity to demonstrate their talent. If somebody wants to make a movie, there's now a way to do it. For years we've heard predictions that the coming of digital tools for filmmaking is going to have a bigger effect on the movies than the coming of sound, or the coming of color, in terms of all the ways that it's going to change filmmaking. Well, it's all very good to have the freedom to tell your story and to be a digital pioneer while you're at it. But will anyone take you seriously?

LEGITIMACY
Will digital image acquisition ever become the standard for the movie industry? Good Machine's vice president of production, Anthony Bregman, thinks the answer is "yes." Bregman was one of the very first champions of digital filmmaking, and produced Nicole Holofcener's *Lovely and Amazing* on 24P HD, using the same kind of camera George Lucas used for *Star Wars: Episode II* to tell a quiet, personal story about a mother and her daughters. He admits that there's still a prejudiced perception that making a film on 35-millimeter is a bigger step than making a feature using a digital camera of any kind — the same kind of prejudice as a theatrical release being more prestigious than an HBO release, even though 10 times as many people see it on HBO.

Five or six years ago it was said that people didn't want to see things shot on video; then it came around to the fact that being done on video *is* cool and people will want to see it *because* it's on video. Now we've come back to people simply asking whether the movie in question has a good story they want to see. But the minute you start relying on digital to *sell* your product because it's technologically cool, you've lost the game. The appeal of a project is still going to stem from its story, though the technology we have today gives filmmakers more tools to tell those stories.

Digital technology also allows for an unprecedented fluidity in the fate of a project. *Gods and Generals*, shot on 35-millimeter film, was originally supposed to be released as a television movie, but as executives became convinced that the feature deserved theatrical distribution, digital intermediate post-production flexibility allowed them to implement this change of plan. The use of digital on projects like *Gods and Generals* raises the bar for what those films can hope to achieve, and keeps options open to produce the best final version of the creative content. Previously, the decision of whether a film would be released theatrically had to be made before the first camera rolled, with a film's destiny pre-ordained all the way through to whether there was a budget for theatrical release or not. Digital dailies and post now allow people to become convinced of a project's theatrical viability midstream. As a result, producers don't have to compromise quality if they change release tactics at the end; they no longer have to drag the project behind a pre-set agenda.

Even so, acquiring digital images is something that's in its infancy, according to Curtis Clark, founder of NeTune Communications, and chairman of the Technology Committee of the American Society of Cinematographers. Despite research and development by leading companies Sony and Thompson, the things that continue to elude digital cameras are the dynamic tonal range, contrast, color-bit depth, and resolution to match those of film. The other thing holding digital back, he says, is the concept of "future-proofing" or archival value. If a producer and director shoot on HD and thereby lock their image into the current digital standard of 1920 x 1080 lines of resolution, the very real danger is that within the next few years, there could be a new standard that would make that obsolete. You'd then have to upgrade to that new standard, and if you shot on film you wouldn't have any problems. If you choose to shoot on film, you're ensuring the value of that product will not be diminished down the road.

This is not to say that sometime down the road, maybe in that five-year window, that digital image capture couldn't rival film. For example, JVC has announced its intention to create a 4K (4,000 lines of resolution) digital camera, and Olympus has a similar prototype. Currently, chip technology offers 2/3-inch image capture CCDs, and cameras are equipped with three separate chips to record red, green, and blue. Olympus's prototype has four chips, two of which are assigned to green because that's where the luminance/contrast capability is. "The ultimate objective would be for a single chip doing RGB with the resolution and size of 35-millimeter," says Clark. "Then the ball game would change." But it's hard to say when those advances will be commercially available, or when post-production capabilities will catch up and be able to work with 4K content as easily as they can with 2K content today.

But if issues of dynamic tonal range, contrast, color bit depth, resolution, and longevity aren't important, then you could use any camera, and make some very interesting movies. You can learn about shot composition, editing, and vital aspects of the process without shooting on film. The question is, *Is digital video good enough for my purposes?* If the whole push is to make the movie in the first place, if it's intended for immediate consumption and not for shelf life, and if the digital origination becomes a virtue and an aesthetic, then of course it is.

There's no question that digital video offers an immediately accessible, and thus very valuable, tool to express the fundamental human behavior of wanting to share experiences and stories. But if visual quality and archival longevity are the standard of what the art and business of film currently are, and you can't get around the longevity thing with digital, is there at least a way to use the visual quality issue to your benefit?

LOOK

For argument's sake, we're going to start out with a generalization and see if we can refute it: Film looks better than digital.

Isn't that what it comes down to, sometimes, in the knee-jerk reactions of moviegoers and executives deciding which films to patronize? Video historically has meant a "flat" look, as opposed to the color gradations and richer grain of images captured on film (to see this contrast, compare a daytime soap opera with a show like *The West Wing*). Mini-DV, which remains the most affordable and widespread consumer camera format, is not even at this TV video broadcast quality. Mini-DV compresses images at a 5-to-1 ratio and only has a limited capacity to register color and luminance from the incoming signal. This means your image resolution and color saturation are going to be much lower than if you shot on more professional formats like digital beta, HD, or film. So when you imagine yourself grabbing an $800 camera and shooting your very own feature movie, keep in mind that it's not going to look anything like what's playing at your local multiplex. We know you already realize that, but steel yourself: it's *really* not going look like a "regular" movie at first.

In a way, people go to the movies because they look like movies. To see something other than themselves, to get lost in the fantasy. And digital isn't there yet. In digital's defense, to throw digital video up on a screen scarcely 10 years after its inception and expect it to instantly rival film may be unfair, as well as unrealistic. Either way, there is still prejudice from people who look at finished digital projects with an eye to financing post, as well as to acquiring or distributing them. In response to the question of whether the word "digital" in the information packet of a film makes him cringe, get happy, or shrug, Lions Gate president of film releasing Tom Ortenberg says, "Personally, these days I still cringe. Because what it likely means is just low-budget. And it's not that we don't like to save money, it's not that we don't like to make our movies for the least amount that we can and still have a great product. But that's still kind of the first instinct."

Even after digital video is transferred to film and corrected for in post, it's very often evident that the original image was shot by a video camera — take *Chuck and Buck*, or *Tadpole*, or many other worthwhile stories that still could never pass for film. But then you see *Lovely and Amazing*, which was shot digitally, but looks like it was made on 35-millimeter film; or *Star Wars: Episode II*, which no one could fault for its filmic visuals. However, both of those were made using 24P high-definition cameras, which match the frames-per-second rate of film and are recording much more information in dynamic tonal range, contrast, color bit depth, and lines of resolution. Our eyes and theater projectors are accustomed to that kind of image quality and the 24fps speed, and the "film look" of digital partially relies on it. Then, what if you're not George Lucas or can't afford a $12,000 a week camera package rental for a 24P Sony HD 900 from Panavision? (Lights are extra). Does this mean that digital looks as good as film for George Lucas, but is going to come out like a home movie for you?

Not necessarily. First of all, there are technologies like Magic Bullet and Filmlook, which were developed for this very reason: there are people who want to conceal the fact that they shot on digital. Not out of embarrassment or anything like that, but out of wanting to present the work in the best possible viewing form.

Filmlook, founded in 1989 by Robert Faber, offers a tape-to-tape process that provides you with a much-improved video version of your movie for either distribution, broadcast, or marketing purposes. Normally, if you shot on film, you would then have to develop the negative, make prints, and do a telecine transfer to get the final film onto a videotape. All pricey. But say you shoot and edit on digital video (best results come from high-resolution formats like Beta or HD, but the process can be applied to any format of digital video) and then take your finished digital movie to Filmlook. Filmlook takes your original tape (usually you'd start the process with a complete, edited master on a digital format like digital beta, or a nearly complete master) to its facility in Burbank, California and makes a new videotape version of it after digitally altering the color contrast, grain texture, and image movement to simulate those of film.

So your end product is still on video, but now it looks like a video copy of something that was shot on film. (This also can be useful if, like Filmlook client PBS, you shoot documentaries that incorporate both archival film footage and also lengthy interviews that were captured on digital video to save money or for logistical ease.) Same result, no film involved, much money saved. In regards to our aesthetic question: if you can get the look of film as your end result, then a difference that makes no difference is no difference, in terms of whether to shoot digital or film. The question is, "Is your digital movie really going to look like film?" Part of that depends on how high the resolution of your original format was, and how well it was lit and shot to begin with. Also, an important caveat is that if you have even a mischievous thought of transferring to film someday, then a process like Filmlook is going to limit your options, since it irrevocably alters your master. If you get the slightest guilty tickle out of thinking that you'd like to see your digital video project as a film output someday, you should talk to a variety of transfer houses before you even roll camera. (Transfers are discussed in Chapter 8; for more on Filmlook and similar processes, visit Chapter 7's discussion of visual effects.)

What about transferring to film to help your digitally shot project look more like film? Some people recommend it. The process of going to film makes the image less static because the grain moves. And it has that little tiny jitter because it's going through a projector. Film prints look great when digitally projected, because they have that grain and jitter, as well as the clarity of the projection system. Going this route naturally adds a great deal of complexity and expense, but can improve the filmic quality of the image, depending on what format you shot on to begin with and how you prepared for the transfer to film.

If you can afford it, the best way to go is to have as much information in the original digital image as possible, which means shooting high-definition. At 1920 lines of resolution, HD is close to the minimum 2000-line standard for 35-millimeter reproduction. The machines that most tape-to-film transfer facilities use right now are 2K film recorders, which means they record at a resolution of 2000 lines. This standard was originally set by technicians who did a bunch of fancy tests to figure out that 2000 lines was the resolving power of the average viewing experience of a print in the theater. People were looking into minimum film resolution for 35-millimeter with the advent of special visual effects that had to be matched to the rest of the film. For instance, a three-second-long laser blast in *Star Wars*, recorded at a 2K resolution, could then be cut back into the rest of the camera negative and look like a seamless shot to the audience. Regardless of what resolution your image starts at, it's brought up to 2K in the film recording process. Sony HD acquires images at 1920 x 1080 lines of resolution. So it's very close to standard film resolution, though there are limitations on the rate that the computer processor can record incoming data onto a DV tape or any other medium.

Does HD look like 35-millimeter? If it's 24P and 1920 lines of resolution, once you transfer it and show it on film, to the untrained eye, it looks almost identical. But if you put a 35-millimeter-originated image up on the screen and show it right after the 24P HD transfer, cinematographers and a lot of producers and directors will see the difference right away in the resolution. Also, video does not have the dynamic range of film in the way that colors and detail register on screen. "All the hype about HD being identical to film, that's the manufacturers talking. The reality is that it's not true," says Digital Film Group founder and president James Tocher.

"Eventually we're going to get to a point where we say, why are we trying so hard anyway, to make video look just like film? Why can't these mediums coexist? But there's a lot of big business behind digital shooting and projection — distribution companies will end up saving the money, but do they want to tell people that it isn't really the same and doesn't really offer the same beauty and aesthetic that we've all come to know and love over the last 100 years?" says Tocher. "Some of the current backlash against digital shooting and projection is from coming to realize that we're being sold a bunch of snake oil, in a way. If advocates of digital video and digital projection had just told people, it's not going to be exactly the same thing as film, then that would have been okay. But the rosy spin on the capabilities of digital video is one reason George Lucas takes flak about trying to sell it to Hollywood. You have to have something that's living up to the promises, because people know the difference."

THE WRAP

> The freedom to tell your story right now, in exactly the way you want do it, can sometimes outweigh concerns about digital video's limited shelf life in the face of rapidly changing technology, as well as concerns about whether its image quality rivals that of film.

> If the look of your movie is your primary concern, consider altering the image in post through software applications or a video-to-film transfer. Your best bet, however, is to accept that digital video will not look precisely like film, and to work with that fact as an aesthetic choice and strength.

> As a rule, it's cheaper and easier to shoot digital. But don't use the inexpensiveness and accessibility as ways to bypass the development process.

> Because they can afford to do it on mini-DV, a lot of people rush into shooting their film, and shortchange themselves by doing it for less money, less marketplace response, and outside support, than they might have been otherwise able to get if they'd developed the material for a longer period.

And developing your story and script is what our next chapter is all about.

chapter
three

>>>*FROM SCRIPT TO CHIP*

When producers and studio executives are asked what they're looking for in projects, they always say they're looking for a good, compelling story. Some will even go so far as to quote the condescending adage, "It's the story, stupid," which has about the same level of truth as the average single man in a bar saying, "What I'm really looking for is a good personality." There may be some validity to the assertion, but the whole picture is more complex than that. As we look at the process of writing a script so that it can be filmed and have an impact on an audience, for just a few moments let's step away from the do-it-yourself-and-who-cares-what-Hollywood-thinks paradigm, because it's (A) good to have some specifics on what you may be rebelling *against*, and (B) maybe secretly you wouldn't be ashamed to get Hollywood interested in your little old script.

In the interest of empowering you as a storyteller, we discuss four strategies that may help you: *understanding* the Hollywood perspective, *telling* your story, *asking* for help, and *thinking inside* the (digital TV) box.

UNDERSTANDING THE HOLLYWOOD PERSPECTIVE
Dispensing with all that blah-blah-blah about story, here are a few of the things that Hollywood is *honestly* looking for.

Casting: Are there name actors already attached — that is, legally agreed and intending to play roles in your script? (A name actor has a name that, if shouted out in a small-town grocery store — for example, "George Clooney is standing in the dairy section!" — would get people scurrying through the aisles to have a look.) If not, do you have roles in the script that a name actor and a really good actor would be excited to play? And it's not just the main role that has to be meaty and well written. If your heroine gets all the good lines, has an unlikable boyfriend and only faces a dumb, uncomplicated villain, there will be trouble finding good (and name) actors for the other roles. The more good actors you have, obviously, the more likely the whole film is to turn out well, and — more to the point in the early stages — the more likely some investor or production company is to pony up the funds to help you get the thing shot.

Other attachments: If you're not going to direct this script yourself (and if you are not already a recognizable director with many pro-duced projects that have been seen on TV and in movie theaters and made money for previous investors), is there a director attached who is going to bring the script prestige and an experienced leadership? Or, is the script of a quality that is going to attract that kind of director? If you've chosen your production crew already, what are their credits? Do you have any financing lined up, any distribution deals in place, any well-known people serving as executive producers or producers? What are the credentials and track records of all those entities? How long has it been since those entities had a successful, profitable film in theaters, and how much profit did they make?

Target audience: Is it immediately obvious, on reading the script, which audience is likely to find this film appealing? Target audiences tend to be labeled in broad categories, such as children and families, women, 18-25 year-old males (this is actually a highly sought-after one, where a lot of the big box office dollars are), and so on. Somewhat corresponding to demographics, this can help you in some cases — for instance, most TV movies-of-the-week are oriented specifically for women who may watch Oprah and be interested in stories of mother-child crises that were torn from this week's headlines. It can also work against your ambitions for a project if, for instance, you really feel your mother-child tearjerker would be best served by theatrical release. Or if your script is about black gang violence, but you need foreign sales to earn back some of your money (historically, black urban movies have not done well outside of the United States). Certain types of stories tend to get pegged as not big enough for the big screen, and the competition for art house distribution and theater space is just as fierce as that for mainstream venues. However, if your script conveys a clear and consistent sense of what kind of crowd is going to fill a theater where your movie is playing, it can only help people decide whether they're interested in helping you get there. "I'm not sure who would ever go see this film" is *not* the reaction you want to get from people who read your script.

Niche markets: One way to make sure that it's obvious who would go see your film is to write it specifically for a niche market. This may limit the project in some aspects, but it may make it much easier to get out to audiences, especially if the initial investment is going to be low in proportion to a built-in word-of-mouth factor from an established, faithful audience. For instance, urban black comedies are seen as a product that can be made for relatively little money and almost guaranteed domestic viewers, especially if there are stars involved. Science fiction lovers, ethnic groups, gay audiences, and horror-film buffs are also treated as core audiences for niche films designed with them in mind. So you might organically come up with a script about a Latina lesbian couple trapped on a haunted asteroid, but you might also structure it with some marketing considerations in mind. The same goes for straight-to-video T & A releases that usually operate off of a quantitative formula of so many bedroom scenes, so many car chases, so many minutes of gratuitous violence, etc. (Did we mention it's a business?) At any rate, television networks, in particular, have institutionalized the niche marketing process by cultivating certain regular audience members. TNT, for instance, specializes in Old West dramas; Lifetime wants women's programming; A&E has an audience for historical romances; PAX looks for wholesome, uplifting stories; Disney and Nickelodeon specialize in children's fare; VH1 original movies always have a popular music component. It makes practical sense because of the advertisers and viewers who keep those channels alive, and you can apply the same marketing principles as your generate your own script.

Anticipated return on investment: This is truly the key. People put money into a film with the hope of getting money back, preferably more money than they started with. Some people want to create art, foster young talent, change society, send a message, tell a story that needs to be told, and so on. And sometimes people are primarily interested in the kind of prestige they can net through working with well-known directors and actors on a project that may not be destined to rake in big bucks. But even those people, if they told the truth, would rather make money than go broke while humoring their ideals. So a lot of elements, starting with the project's cast and audience, go into the perception of its anticipated return on investment. If an agent, producer, distributor, financier, or your rich Aunt Sally looks at your script and dollar signs start to spin in their pupils because the casting potential is obvious and the story is so compelling that people are going to stampede the theaters to go watch this movie, then that's a good start in getting people to respond favorably when you ask them to get involved in financing the production of your movie.

Granted, you may not give a rat's behind about any of the above. You may be considering digital for the very reason that it enables you to adopt this liberated attitude. And that nonconformist spirit is commendable, and fostering it is one of the great and exciting things about the emergence of digital cinema. But unless you only hope to play your completed movie for you yourself alone, it's worth knowing about the above as you craft your overall vision and finished product.

TELLING YOUR STORY

Now for the story itself, which is, despite our cynical demurs above, exceedingly important. If you're having trouble deciding what story you want to tell, there are any number of writing books available to help you with creative tips, brainstorming exercises, heartfelt wisdom, and so on. Our best advice in a nutshell is to find a theme you care about and have something to say about, make sure all the elements of the story serve that theme, develop your characters to the point where the best actors in the world would be thrilled to play them, and keep in mind your target audience and the impact you want your story to have on them. This is true for a dramatic story in any medium.

From the standpoint of a do-it-yourself digital production, some people think it's better to start with the resources you have (Robert Rodriguez knew he had access to a dog and a bar, and both became featured in his legendary microbudget film, *El Mariachi*) and build the story outwards from there. Other people find that method creatively stunting, and would rather start by coming up with a good story first and then simplifying its elements afterwards.

In other words, group two might start out with an epic science fiction action spectacular, find that the epic was actually about a very simple conflict or theme — say, betrayal, as seen in one man's moral dilemma and his choice to abandon his friends in order to side with those in power when the going got rough. Then, group two would find a way to explore that theme of betrayal with the same basic character actions, but on a smaller scale, such as in the parking garage of their apartment building, with three actors instead of three armies, and during the day (so they didn't have to rent lights). In contrast, group one would find someone who already owned a spaceship, and take it from there. Both approaches are valid.

Take the experience of writer-director Roy Finch, whose digital feature *Wake* starred Martin Landau and a cast of unknowns ("unknowns" certainly doesn't equal inexperienced or untalented; in Hollywood terms, it just means that these actors' names, shouted out in the grocery store, would prompt no reaction from shoppers). His whole script was tailored to be shot digitally. "I had a script that I'd worked on for about two and a half years, and had some big names attached — Martin Landau, Benjamin Bratt — but a lot of the feedback I was getting was, 'The script's good, you have a great cast, but you've never shot a film before — why should we trust you with six million dollars?' And so I just thought, I can't wait around in L.A. for somebody to say, 'Here,' and give me the money. *Do something, anything,* was my mantra, rather than waiting around. Then, we were visiting Maine and we saw this house, and I said, 'That looks like an incredible set. What took place in a house like that?' So that's pretty much how it came about. There was an old guy living in that house for like forty-five years, never painted, never left the house." So Finch wrote a script for the location once the deal on the house went through (he and his wife wanted to buy it anyway), and while he developed the main characters he also kept in mind some of the actors he knew and wanted to work with.

However you get your inspiration, it is absolutely critical to make sure your script is ready before going out to shoot it. Staged readings, videotaped rehearsals, and storyboarding (or previsualization animation, if you have access to the technology and know-how) can all help pre-edit the script by showing what dialogue, staging, and camera moves are truly necessary to get the point across. But even so, it's a fact of production that many scenes will end up on the cutting room floor (or dragged into the Trash icon, these days). Often, this is because writers and directors were so tied to unnecessary scenes that they kept them in the script, and used days and days to shoot them, when any of the above tools would have proved that those scenes were dead weight that needed to be dropped.

Also, if you want to use improvisation, it eats up time but sometimes allows you to discover things that weren't on the page. So when you're writing a script to be shot via down-and-dirty guerrilla filmmaking, it's to your benefit to give yourself more time than you think you need. Take a single page of any script, and see how long it takes you to shoot it with adequate coverage of all the actors in a conversation, an establishing shot of the location, close-ups of relevant action, reaction shots, and masters. Factor in camera setups, lighting changes, blocking rehearsals (for camera, not for performance), multiple takes, and the million things that can go wrong in your own backyard, let alone anyplace outside it, and then think long and hard about whether you really want to use 10-point Times font and 1/2" page margins on your script. This is assuming you're not using costumes, sets, makeup, extras, cars, children, animals, or sound. Don't crunch those pages.

ASKING FOR HELP

Another thing you can do to help yourself and your project is to get feedback on the script. Be selective about who you show your work to, and know yourself whose feedback you'll receive less objectively (for example, from your spouse, your mother, your arch-rival from film school), and therefore, whose feedback is going to be the most useful at any given stage of writing. Also be aware that people may be bringing emotional baggage and competitive streaks to their interpretation of your work, and that you are as much a fool to listen to *everyone's* advice as you are a fool to listen to no one's advice.

Before you show your work to someone else, make sure you have enough emotional distance from it so that you don't take criticisms and suggestions as personal insults or threats to your integrity and worth as an artist. If people are gracious enough to give you feedback, don't sass back at them with your opinion of their opinions, or give flippant or hostile replies to questions about what the feedback-givers consider problematic in your script. Think these snappy rejoinders in your head all you want, but outwardly show respect to people, and they will be much more likely to give you more help (such as further advice or referrals) or give the next person help. Don't disregard the wheel of karma here.

And if you're presenting your script to people in the hope of getting them to help you directly — whether with their money, their connections, or their own talents and labor — this principle applies as well: you have one shot to make the best impression possible on a reader. If you can't spell and suddenly wrap up all your loose plot threads in the last five pages, don't expect that your brilliance will show through. Although there is a lot to be said for the screenwriting advice books that tell you to make the first five pages amazing, gripping, spectacular, and so forth, it's also true that the best first five pages in the world won't save you from the common weaknesses of passive heroes, rambling dialogue, novelistic scene directions, one-dimensional villains and sidekicks, unconvincing romances, implausible plot twists, and anticlimactic conclusions. And even in the case where your story is great, frequent spelling mistakes, grammatical errors, and unprofessional formatting can dampen the enthusiasm of a reader being asked to vouch for you. Spell-check is not enough. If you have not recently won a spelling bee, do your script a favor and have someone other than yourself proofread it. Sounds petty, but it's not. Try this: Scarlett O'Hara clutches at Rhett Butler in the doorway, asking where will she go, what will she do, and he replies, "Frankly, my deer, I don't give a damn." Takes you out of the moment a bit, doesn't it?

When you convince a person in the film industry to read your script and give you feedback, understand that the more well-connected and busy someone is, the more likely he is to get someone else to read your script for him. Say you got your foot in the door at a production company because you met a producer in the buffet line after a friend's screening, and you asked if the producer would read your script, and the producer answered with a cordially enthusiastic, *Sure, send it over to my office, I'm always looking for a good story.* First of all, the producer usually won't read the script. Generally what happens is that your script, like the five to 50 others that arrived that week, will be sent off for the weekend read. Fine, so you picture some earnest reader turning off the phone and sitting in a silent room for an uninterrupted afternoon to pore over your script, cover to cover, while bending the full weight of her well-developed analytical powers onto your script's merits and intentions, independent of any other considerations except for the art that you have meticulously crafted and poured your heart and soul into for the last six months.

Here's the first sad truth: readers skim. Especially if in the first 30 pages or so (some people say in the first five, but 30 is a little fairer) your script is not really going anyplace interesting, new, or focused (the latter being for those cases when the reader has read 30 pages of dialogue and still has not seen the main character encounter an actual problem or change in his life). If you're a relative unknown and the reader doesn't have expectations of your work, she won't give it automatic credit because it doesn't have name actors or producers attached; and, as a stranger to you and the person who recommended you, she won't have any extra pressure on her to seriously consider the script. And one thing about skimming is that if nothing is really happening in your script, it becomes very evident in a skim. Think of how you could watch a movie on fast-forward and get a sense of the overall amount of action or lack thereof.

Next sad truth: This reader may be some combination of overworked, underpaid, distracted by other tasks and pursuits, extremely short on time (which means he may have to pick up and put down your magnum opus half a dozen times over the course of a weekend or a week or a month), and prejudiced against other writers because he is a struggling writer, too. This reader may even be an unpaid intern with little or no experience evaluating scripts. Painful but true, your months of labor, craft, and passion may get passed on (in Hollywood, "passing" on something means giving it the big thumbs down) by a nineteen year-old college student — a student who is working at that company for a summer because some mid-level staff member owed his mother a favor — because he's not a fan of science-fiction epics or themes of betrayal, or because in his pile of seven scripts to take home that weekend, there were three science fiction epics about betrayal, and he couldn't recommend all three without looking like a total geek. There is an element of random chance when you're arriving with the masses, and that's just the way it is.

On the other hand, some readers are very sharp and very fair, and will read every word you have written. This is when it becomes extremely important for your script to be properly formatted, without typos or spelling errors, and really damn good. Because like everyone else in the process, readers are under pressure to justify their paychecks and their discerning taste to those further up the food chain. You don't know what hassles and personality conflicts the reader may be dealing with in his or her production company or daily life. So if the reader is going to go out on a limb to recommend your script, that reader wants to be sure to come out looking good as a result. Imagine that the reader is setting her boss up on a blind date. The reader is going to make sure this potential Mister or Miss Right is not going to reflect badly on *her*. Readers will not recommend scripts that could come back to haunt them in embarrassing ways. Embarrassing includes getting fired for having bad taste or sensibilities that just don't match those of the company as a whole.

To avoid this kind of unhappy outcome, readers don't just evaluate a script for how good the story is. They also look at character development, structure, pacing, tone, thematic message, emotional impact, castability, marketability, audience appeal, and suitability for the production entity for which they work. Often, coverage (which is essentially a book report about the script in question) will compare the screenplay to other movies, in order to give the next person up the food chain a quick snapshot of what the script would be like as a movie. It's not the Hollywood stereotype of "It's *Jaws* meets *Annie*;" instead, it's a way to provide an instant frame of reference for the reader's brief synopsis and commentary — for example, "This script has the period style and brooding tone of *L.A. Confidential*, though its hero is on the other side of the law."

Naturally, you want your script to evoke emotionally powerful, well-made, and financially successful movies (this is not to say it will be imitative; it's just the nature and shorthand of people in the film industry to put your movie somewhere in the spectrum of others that have come before it). So while at a certain point, you have to cut the umbilical cord and go out into the world and onto the set with your script, it is in your interest to do as much as possible to refine your script before that happens. A good refining exercise is to analyze the screenplay of your favorite movie, and think about why its characters and events affect you. Make a note of the pace, be aware of how much information is conveyed in a scene, and notice how much information and character change is conveyed without any words at all. Then tell your own story in pictures. In actions. In events. In settings. In changing internal emotions. In other words, don't fall so in love with the fact that you can shoot your story that you jump into physical production before the script is ready. All the inexpensive digital takes in the world won't fix a character who was only ever written to be an unlikable one-dimensional caricature of an unchallenging villain.

Once you start showing your baby around, should you even advertise that you intend to shoot the script on digital video? Depends on the circumstances. If you are approaching people for production money or people to work as cast and crew members, then yes, you should be honest and clear about your intentions. DV doesn't have the stigma it used to, and lying to people you want money and labor from can only get you into trouble in the long run. However, if you are simply shopping your this-could-be-done-on-DV feature script as a writing sample or with the secret hope that someone will see that the only way to do justice to this particular story would be on 35-millimeter film — then it is not to your benefit to pigeonhole yourself as either a digital video screenwriter *or* a film writer. If it gets that far, a line producer or similarly skilled person will budget out your script for film, as well as for a variety of digital formats to see what would work best for the money on hand. And unless you are dead set on using digital because of your aesthetic choices or production needs, it's totally worthwhile to compare the numbers.

THINKING INSIDE THE (DIGITAL TV) BOX
What if you secretly want to write for television? Is there such a thing as a digital marketplace for television scripts? Well, yes and no. Most television shows that are shooting on digital are doing so for reasons of budget or technical decisions; the format of the script, and the various peaks and cliffhangers and minute-lengths for commercial break purposes don't have anything to do with that. If you want to write for TV, you don't need to write with digital image acquisition in mind.

That said, there is an entirely different route to consider in television, and that is high-definition TV, or HDTV. You've seen the goggle-eyed men entranced by football games and Rolling Stones concerts on those giant, crystal-clear, color-popping screens at Circuit City and Best Buy. They're watching high-definition images designed to maximize the impact of the newest-fangled big-screen televisions. Yes, the pictures are very sharp and pretty. Yes, they impress your friends. This is what Mark Cuban, founder of HD Net, is counting on. As more and more households switch over to non-analog television sets with HD capabilities, Cuban sensibly predicts, those viewers will naturally want to turn to channels that broadcast HD content to fully enjoy the benefits of their upwardly mobile TV purchases. With this in mind, Cuban started HD Net to broadcast hi-def content on three HD channels that feature sports, movies, and concerts, respectively.

Since high-definition television broadcasting is a relatively untapped field, there's a lot of room for brand-new product created by digitally savvy folks such as you. The reason for the welcome is that while there's a vast quantity of television programming that originated on tape, those tape masters are unusable for HD broadcast, and the large amount of product out there that originated on analog film, while usable, is very expensive to digitally re-master.

"I'm looking for eye candy," Cuban says cheerfully, explaining that his average customer, Joe Six-Pack — "and I say that with all the love in my heart" — wants to show his new HD television off to his buddies while kicking back and enjoying the vibrant, crystal-clear images on his big screen. For Cuban, this means lots of great visual content, and the fledgling nature of his company means that he feels no need to sink excess capital into purchasing the rights to broadcast that content. Bikini contests, for instance, nicely fit this low-production-cost-to-high-eye-candy-ratio. On the plus side for content providers, Cuban has no objections to letting creators sell their analog rights in any other market, and this is one thing he offers when producing live events (sports, concerts, and so on) and giving the performers, for instance, an HD master and production facilities in return for replay rights. He makes it clear that he is looking for completed product, since he does not provide a budget for finishing funds.

So, what this means to you as a writer for the digital market is that you could script and shoot (on HD, since remastering from film is expensive, and consumer or prosumer-level digital video is a compressed format that would look awful if broadcast on a high-definition output) a story about a bikini-clad touch football game, and bring the finished product to Mark Cuban to try to sell him the digital broadcast rights, while keeping the analog rights to sell to buyers in other markets.

THE WRAP

> People always say that they're just looking for good stories, but what they're really looking for are anticipated return on investments, cast and creative attachments, target audiences, and niche markets.

>The reason people say they're looking for good stories is that a compelling, well-told story is still one of the determining factors in a movie's success from start to finish.

> When you rally outside support for your script, be ruthless in rewriting and refining the script to its full potential, and be professional in how you present yourself and your work. Hollywood relies on first impressions, and even outside of Hollywood, you usually get exactly one shot with each person you approach.

> One way to try to make money on your stories is to keep in mind who will be willing to pay to see them, whether a specialized content distributor such as HD Net or a niche audience member standing in line outside a theater.

Now that we've filled your mind with visions of high art and the ways that the digital process can enable you to share your stories, it's time to get to the *real* process enablers: money and hardware.

chapter
four

>>>CHEAPER, FASTER... BETTER?

"There is no strength in one person," said director Mike Figgis in a 1997 interview. "There is tremendous strength in five people working together." What he meant was that with the right collaboration of talent, plus a digital videocamera, "there's no reason anyone can't make a feature on digital right now." That was a startling assertion at the time, but it has been proved true over and over again in the years since then. No one doubts today that digital is an immediately accessible tool to tell stories. Furthermore, digital doesn't have to look or behave like film in order for you to use it as a compelling creative and aesthetic choice. So these days, if you have a story, there's no reason for you not to use digital images to tell it.

To empower yourself to tell your story with the tools that are best for your vision and resources, get acquainted with the distinctions among the various digital formats available to consumers, "prosumers," and professionals (although what makes you a professional in this sense is nothing other than your purchasing power). There are many subdivisions of different kinds of tapes and accompanying equipment in each, most of which are not at all mutually compatible. This can create significant expense and hassle for post-production houses, which have to accommodate all different types of incoming formats while adhering to various broadcast-standard formats. But here is a basic primer on formats and image resolution available to the populace at large:

> Mini-DV: On lower-end camcorders, the image is heavily compressed, at a ratio of 5-to-1, in order to save space in recording data. If you then burn a DVD of your DV footage, you get another compression ratio of about 5-to-1, which looks about five times worse than what you started out with.

> You'll also see digital cameras in this and other categories rated with numbers like 4:1:1 and 4:2:2. What the heck does that mean? Cameras in the previous category sample half as much digital information in the luminance and chrominance channels, and transfer the image data to tape half as fast, often with much more compression. Cameras in the latter category provide a more "robust signal," a better image, and more information for manipulation in post-production and film transfers. They also cost more.

> If a camera has three CCDs and not just one, it will give you better color rendition. This is because the camera gains more control over the color matrix by separating color into red, green, and blue components instead of registering all three via one CCD. For your thumbnail reference, the CCD (charge coupled device) itself is the part where light goes in, and ones and zeroes come out.

> A true 16:9 CCD is itself shaped with the slightly broader width-to-height ratio of a movie screen, as opposed to the cheaper, 4:3, TV-screen ratio of other CCDs. True 16:9 CCDs allow you to capture images in that aspect ratio without resorting to "squeezed" (also known as anamorphic) 16:9 to pack digital information in, and without framing your 4:3 viewfinder for 16:9, which also doesn't produce as desirable a result.

> Other prosumer DV ranges from Digital Betacam — recording in 4:2:2 color, much less compression (2 to 1), 90 Mbps data and 10 bits per sample — to the D-9 and DVC Pro 50 formats. These also register color in a 4:2:2 ratio, and have a faster data rate (50 Mbps) and less compression (3.3 to 1). They have 8 bits per sample, like lower-end DV formats. DV formats also have a slower data rate at 25 Mbps, and only get 4:1:1 color.

> Also, if any of these cameras is shooting interlaced fields of video, which they're probably doing unless "progressive" is included in the camera's specifications, then the lines of resolution in every frame are being treated as two separate groups. First one group, or field, is refreshed, and then the other. Each field changes every 1/60th of a second, so by the time 1/30th of a second passes, the entire frame has been refreshed. These are the interlaced fields that have to be de-interlaced before you can do a transfer to film; it's one more thing to consider in choosing a shooting format.

> High-definition has 1920 horizontal lines of resolution. Unless a format specifies that it is HD, you can safely assume it to be standard-definition (the normal stuff that the ordinary consumer would have, in other words). Standard-definition doesn't mean low-resolution or low-quality necessarily; for instance, Digital Betacam is standard-definition, and is also used for network TV broadcast and mastering.

> A camera with 24P in its name means that it captures images at twenty-four frames per second to match the rate of film. The "P" stands for progressive, which means that unlike an interlaced video stream, this progressive video stream does not split each frame's lines of resolution into two fields. Instead, the entire frame is renewed every 1/60th of a second, which means you get better picture quality.

> 24P HD: George Lucas used this to shoot *Episode II: Attack of the Clones.* 24 frames per second like a film camera, with progressive video stream, and high-definition resolution.

> 24P mini-DV is a much newer category, which brings us full circle to what is available to the widest consumer market. This standard-definition, compressed format may not give you the resolution, color range and data content of other cameras, but

at least it will take one step out of a transfer to film, and may help you achieve a more filmic look without some of the more expensive kinds of post-production manipulation.

It's been said that digital cinema is the intersection of technology and desire, where people get to participate as much as they are inspired, instead of before, when most people could only admire from the sidelines. The flip side of that accessibility and ease is that more people than ever before are rushing into shooting their films before the script is ready. In addition to developing the script and rehearsing with actors, it can give your digital project a huge boost to work with technical advisors at post-production houses and film transfer facilities in order to get advice on lighting setups, camera lenses and filters, and general pitfalls of production. A director of photography who has experience acquiring images digitally also will make a huge difference in the visual style and impact of your feature or short. It may be that you want to be your own cinematographer, or that your cinematographer has worked mostly on analog formats before now and wants to team up with you for the sake of getting digital experience. Either way, it's always worth your while to research new technologies and practices, even if you intend to shoot guerrilla-style on a shoestring budget.

And there's no denying that the original impetus to shoot DV came from the fact that it was, and is, a cheaper way to tell a visual story. Digital video's sensitivity to light eliminates the need for costly lighting packages and the people to operate them; filmmakers can move fast with tiny or nonexistent crews, shooting continuously on inexpensive tapes that can last over 90 minutes. The first widely acclaimed movie to take advantage of this mobility was *Celebration* by director Thomas Vinterberg, who shot the project under most of the strict practical guidelines of the Dogme 95 pact he helped establish — available light, no soundtrack music, no alteration or decoration of sets, using only existing locations, and so on (ironically, Dogme 95 also specified 35-millimeter film as the chosen medium). More recent films are continuing this bare-bones trend; for instance, *Boxes* is getting national distribution on the Independent Film Channel after being shot on DV for $285. This included $150 for haircuts, a charge added on after a good friend of the hairdresser's did not receive a promised role in the movie. Effects are very simple, but funny, and DV suits the fast-moving, conversational, in-your-face style of Rene Alberto Gil's movie about the hassles and rituals of dating.

Digital can also be a way for new directors to be discovered. Craig Brewer used a digital video camera and a novice crew to shoot *The Poor and the Hungry*, a documentary-style feature about how chop shops disassemble your car, save the parts, have the frame towed to a police auction, buy the frame legally for about $80, and then reassemble your car, which they now legally own and even have the pink slip for. He's now making his next feature with Focus. Director of *Monster's Ball* Marc Forster made his first feature, *Everything Put Together*, on digital. This unsettling film follows the emotional and mental breakdown of a woman who lost her baby, and its fast edits, jarring sequences and intense performances would have been much more costly and difficult to capture on film. In that movie, continuous and numerous takes on digital helped actors and directors stay in character and in the moment, allowing them to show their stuff without the cost of film stock or printing. Digital technology also allows storytelling in environments that ordinarily would have been prohibitively inhospitable, such as the Arctic, where some crewmembers of the Inuit tale *The Fast Runner* were in charge of hunting for food, literally.

Directors working with digital video cameras report an exhilarating creative experience. From a practical standpoint, choosing digital over film can suddenly allow room in your budget for drastically higher shooting ratios as well as luxuries like dolly and Steadicam shots. This is not to say that film will go away in a hurry or even ever, but that new technology is becoming more affordable and transparent. With a wider array of choices available, digital origination becomes a personal choice for what you want to do with your project.

Then there's the question of whether to own or rent the camera. The short answer is that unless you are a cinematographer renting your equipment along with your services, it may not make economic sense to invest significant money (between $1,000 and $50,000) on an item that will almost certainly be outdated a year or two from the purchase date. For example, the introduction of the Panasonic 24P mini-DV (the AG-DVX 1000, which costs roughly $3500 and rents for $350 a day) means that everyone who went out and spent $5000 on the PD 150 a year or two ago is seeing that there's an even spiffier toy on the market now.

On the other hand, owning your camera can allow for improvisation over time with actors; meanwhile, you can edit for several weeks, and then six months later revise the script and do a significant re-shoot, or small re-shoots along the way. And when you own a camera and have that kind of time, you can master the craft. When you rent, you're under enormous pressure to return it all by Monday morning, and you may be forced to compromise the shooting process as a result.

Veteran cinematographer, and head of Digital Film Group transfer house, James Tocher says that when shopping around for cameras, don't just go by the hype and the price. Hype is generated by manu-facturers selling product; even Internet chat rooms comparing digital video cameras may only be populated by consumers who have read the manufacturers' literature and not field-tested the cameras them-selves. Prices happen for a great variety of reasons, including but cer-tainly not limited to: how good the camera's internal software is for taking digital samples from what the lens shows to the CCD chips; how good the CCD chips themselves are; how good the lens is; and how well the camera imaging system allows those variables to interact. Cameras are changing so rapidly that you should consult regularly with cinematographers and camera operators who constantly test technology from both a creative and a technical standpoint. And even they can't predict future developments.

Take the 24P mini-DV camera. It represents a possibility for people who want to blow up to film and, for the present, it's a viable choice. But in the next six months, someone else may have something better, with higher resolution, for only a little more money. And people who buy those 24P mini-DV cameras will have an expectation that they're ahead of the crowd because they can shoot 24P, but, actually, all the mini-DV limitations of CCD size, compression, and color contrast still apply.

Once you gather an understanding of the basics and differences in these cameras, it's still best to go to the experts to get the fine points of pros and cons in performance and image quality. These days, producers and directors are becoming more technically informed and they want to know more, but the cinematographer should still be the one entrusted with the in-depth knowledge of what tool is best for the project at hand. Directors can go back to their original job of deciding what aesthetic is going to allow them to tell their story the way they want to tell it, and then delegating the technical know-how to the cinematographer. This is especially true for do-it-yourself filmmakers whose primary interest is in storytelling.

In addition to knowing why various cameras are producing a variety of types of images, your cinematographer can shoot test footage from multiple cameras to help you evaluate those images for what they are. On one level, it's not whether you know the technical specifications or what manufacturers tell you about how many lines of resolution are being recorded, and it doesn't even matter what size the camera's CCD is — in the end it only matters what your *eye sees*.

Imagine that you've been presented with a variety of microphones to record sound. You'd want to test the results of each microphone in the particular setting for what you want: are you recording an argument in a bathroom, or a piano recital in a packed concert hall, or someone's footsteps walking through a peaceful forest? You'd probably find that each microphone had different strengths and weaknesses in each environment. Likewise, cameras will perform differently in different circumstances, and the more specific your vision is for your desired end result, the more tests you'll want to do with variables that mimic your shooting situation as closely as possible.

Even with the manufacturers' hype, people know there has to be a difference between a $3500 24P mini-DV versus the $150,000 24P HD camera that George Lucas uses (you would hope that you'd get something more for the extra $146,500). But even the high-end cameras are not going to give you the same result as film. And if you don't assume that these cameras are going to capture film-like images, you'll have no reason to be disappointed. Film is, by comparison, easier to shoot than video to get a pleasing aesthetic result, so where video works best is in situations where people are not so obsessed with the image itself, and are more interested in telling a story. At that point you just need to balance your storytelling with enough technical knowledge so that you don't make unnecessary sacrifices in resolution or picture quality. You should also understand that what you see on the monitor does not equal what you're going to see projected on a screen or transferred to film; again, get help from people more technically experienced than yourself, or get your own technical experience on the way to shooting your project.

A few more tips for choosing a camera: the camera lens is crucial in affecting your image's overall sharpness, chromatic aberrations, and light sensitivity — correspondingly, compare lenses (ideally in consultation with an experienced and objective cinematographer) for glass quality, lens shape, and speed.[2] If you go to Pro DV's bigger 2/3" CCD with true 16:9 capability, you are rewarded with greater resolution than you would have been by choosing something smaller-chipped and non-16:9, like a Canon XL1 or Sony PD150. Cameras in the 4:2:2 category, which record to a tape format like Digital Betacam or DVCPRO50, theoretically have twice the resolution and color reproduction capability of the 4:1:1 formats.[3] Unsportingly, they cost way more than twice as much.

---

[2]"The Truth Is In What You See," James Tocher, RES Magazine, January/February 2001
[3]"Upping the Image Ante: Professional DV Cameras and Transferring to Film," James Tocher, RES Magazine, January/February 2002

Currently, here are some of the top rental (or purchase, if you have between $10,000 and $50,000 plus sales tax to throw around) standard-definition, interlaced digital video camera choices. Technology is moving fast in developing newer, faster, and smarter cameras, but the following models all share baseline features of 2/3" true 16:9 CCDs and interchangeable lenses (most prosumer cameras have 1/2" or 1/3" CCDs, including the 24P mini-DV from Panasonic).

Sony DSR500

Very sensitive to light, with DCC and Dynalatitude signal processing, this camera will give you more detail in the white areas that typically get blown out on video. The low-light sensitivity comes from signal boosting that could also result in grainy blacks; to hide that graininess, the camera tends to crush the blacks. Used to shoot *The Anniversary Party*, this 4:1:1 Pro DV camera costs about $16,000 and supports DVCAM and mini-DV tape formats. If you're renting, this camera has a list price of $500 a day. But it's a standard rental house practice to offer a 30% discount, which results in a $350 a day weekend rental, meaning pickup Friday afternoon and return on Monday morning.

JVC DV700

A newer entrant in the camera races, this was partly designed with the blow-up to film in mind. Totally different innards from the DSR 500 offer you more detail in uncrushed blacks, but not quite as much sensitivity to light. It also controls highlights, but enhances details automatically, so you'll want to turn that default setting down to avoid getting those telltale halo effects if you transfer to film. For roughly $10,000, this Pro DV camera will allow you to acquire 4:1:1 images on mini-DV (that's also a cheaper tape format than the others listed here). As a daily rental this would have the same price as the DSR 500: $350 after the discount.

Panasonic AJ-D610

A 4:1:1 Pro DV camera, this shoots DVCPRO and mini-DV tapes for about $14,000. It has about the same light sensitivity as the DV700, and Panasonic has historically gone for better color response than its competitors. Rental: $350 a day.

Sony DVW-790WS (WS stands for widescreen)

Digital Betacam gets you broadcast quality with 4:2:2 capabilities, but you could also put a down payment on a nice house for that $40 to $50,000. This camera gets gorgeous images straight out of the camera (take a look at the exterior sequences in *Dancer in the Dark*) through highlight control, high resolution and the advantages of Sony R & D. It also sports pre-sets for different lighting scenarios so that you can move locations and setups faster. You can crush blacks, lighten reds, darken blues and so on; assuming you have a cinematographer or engineer who can get you the right results, it would be like doing your own onsite telecine. Rental: $750 a day.

JVC DY-90U

Shooting D9, or Digital S, this 4:2:2 camera costs a slightly less hair-raising $22,000. It also allows you to record four tracks of audio, and up to 124 minutes per D9 tape. As sensitive to low light as the JVC DV700, it also has very good detail in black areas and is set up to give you the best film transfer material possible. Rental: $350 a day. (All the smaller-end DV cameras are about the same where rentals are concerned.)

Panasonic AJ-PD900

For its DVCPRO50 format and its 4:2:2 rating, you'll pay around $37,000. You also get the ability to record to tape in 4:1:1 as well as in a mode called DVCPRO "P", which produces 60 progressive frames per second. This benefits you if and when you transfer to film because you'll have fewer interlacing artifacts to deal with.[4]

---

[4]"Upping the Image Ante: Professional DV Cameras and Transferring to Film," James Tocher, *RES Magazine*, January/February 2002

Remember that the 4:2:2 category is going to give you more color and resolution than a 4:1:1 mini-DV, even if your 4:1:1 mini-DV is the 24P kind. As Tocher says, little and cheap usually looks little and cheap no matter how you slice it. You can get a better quality if you rethink the budget a little bit and turn camera purchases into camera rentals.

And if you do rent, it can really be worth your while to rent the higher-end cameras listed above by spending $750 a day instead of $350. After all, you get about $40,000 more worth of camera. What you spend on the 790 gets you a great quality picture — you'd have to spend the money in post to get the same quality out of a DSR 500. You want to shoot with the highest and best quality you can, obviously.

We asked Jeff Shapiro, vice president of World Wide Broadcast Services, for his advice on equipment rentals for digital productions. The average lighting package for a modest DV shoot is going to be the same as if you were lighting for a high-definition feature or a 35-millimeter film (if you're thinking documentary, a small package suitable for an indoor interview would be much less, say $100 for a four- to six-light Arri kit). The average dramatic indoor and outdoor feature requires a much bigger lighting setup, in the ballpark of $1000-$1500 a day for a modest package of HMI lights on down, as well as all the supporting gear. Keep in mind that it's not just the lights you're paying for — you need stands to put those lights on, sandbags to weigh the stands down so they don't tip over, cables to connect the lights to power sources, scrims and dimmers and flags and bounces so that you have more lighting choices than On and Off; the list goes on and on. *But wait*, you say, *I just wanted to take my little camera out and shoot in existing light, or with a couple of lights. I didn't want to be renting sandbags for three dollars a pop.* Don't be alarmed, we're not saying you have to go fill up a grip truck with rented equipment. We just want you to know the spectrum of options so that you make your choices in context rather than just out of following the crowd.

A high-definition camera is $1200 a day to rent, and if you want a 24P HD camera it's $1500 each day. Along with the camera, Shapiro's rental company will throw in with that package price an 8-inch Sony color monitor, a 15 x 8 zoom lens, four camera batteries, a tripod, a power supply, and charger; also, they'll include a $100 lighting kit and field mixers, a headset, fishpole, shotgun, and lapel microphones. If you want a 13" high-resolution monitor to give you more accurate feedback of what you're capturing on set, that's $50 a day. To get any of these rentals, you first need to show a certificate of insurance from an insurance agent. This insurance covers $100,000 for the camera, lighting and sound package. Usually, it costs $500 a week for the certificate, which insures the rental company against loss, damage, and downtime for repair. If you're shooting on HD, up that insurance to $250,000. If you're in film school, you may be in luck; check to see if you are automatically covered under your school's liability insurance policy.

In favor of renting versus owning, let's say you bought the DigiBeta 790 from the list above. You've spent $40,000, and in the middle of your production the camera suddenly stops working. You have to send the camera back to a Sony dealer, and then wait anywhere from two days to a few weeks to get the parts in. And even if it's only two days, maybe those were the only two days you had with a certain actor before he flew off to Micronesia to star in another movie. But if you had rented that camera and it died on you, you'd make a phone call, and in an hour you'd have another camera on the tripod.

Shapiro's personal favorite for the lower-end digital cameras is the Sony DSR PD150. "It's the camera I have on the front seat of my car. Once, I was driving, and I saw this guy on a Harley — and it's November. And he weighs about 400 pounds, and he's in a pair of shorts. He's got the plumber's crack, and his gut hanging out, and he was just enjoying himself, and it's this bright yellow Harley, and I just had to shoot him. Things like that. As a producer and a filmmaker myself, I'm always looking for things that make me laugh, that spark my creativity. Hey, I mean, if I could have a 24P hi-def camera on my front seat, I would. But with a little camera you can throw your jacket over it and go into a store and nobody knows that it's there." The PD 150 has lots of nifty ways to customize the look of your image, a video-screen that flips out instead of forcing you to squint through a viewfinder, and true 16:9 CCD; you can change frame rates, capture in progressive mode and so forth. Also, you can FireWire this camera's data straight into your computer just like you can with the other ones.

Whatever you choose for your equipment and however you get hold of it, you can preserve the Dogme spirit in your shoot. Digital and Dogme both foster a back-to-the-basics approach to filmic storytelling, which is, in a way, a rebirth of the French New Wave movement. The French New Wave was similar to the Dogme aesthetic in that it was after a less Hollywoodized cinema, with camera techniques that were aggressive rather than transparent (the use of the camera in *Breaking the Waves* was aggressive, making you conscious of its movement and angles as an active part of the storytelling style and effect; the use of the camera in *Home Alone* was transparent). New Wave films were shot on location instead of in artificial studio settings, and came out of the work of writer-directors whose vision was externalized by the camera in the same way that a novelist's vision was set forth with a pen (or a word processor) — in other words, in an active and uniquely personal way.

Like computer animators who can benefit from a background in art history and figure drawing you, as a digital filmmaker, can benefit from understanding the historical context of what you're doing when you step outside with your mini-DV camera and extra battery in hand. At the same time, no matter what camera is in your hand, you'll benefit from exploring the medium for what it is instead of thinking how you can force it to look like film. You can try to get what you like and exploit digital's strengths, but also you have to respect video's limitations.

And just because you can shoot the movie and do all the sound your-self doesn't mean you should. Technical knowledge helps a director, but nothing can replace the experience and skill that the right cinematographer can bring — even though with digital video, cinematographers have lost some perceived value on set, which has also happened for other technical and creative positions. The video medium is a lot more collaborative than film, and on a digital video shoot, with designated technicians tweaking the equipment at every turn, the cinematographer can't say she's the only one who knows whether the exposure and lighting ratio is right, whereas in a film production the shot might look odd on set, but look great after the footage has been to the lab because the cinematographer really knows what she's doing.

All the other things that make a movie work visually, such as the lighting and aesthetic approach, are the same as in film. But if a cinematographer really understands what he or she doing technically, it behooves you to take that DP's advice. As James Tocher says, "If I'm a DP and I say your movie has a lot of wide shots, and to accommodate those you should go for a higher resolution camera, and you say, *But I love this little camera* — at some point you should say, *Maybe he's got something here.* Nine times out of 10 you'll be happy you listened to an experienced DP, and unhappy if you didn't listen."

THE WRAP

> Work with experienced cinematographers and technical advisors at post-production houses and film transfer facilities in order to arm yourself with as much knowledge as possible before going into production.

> Having done that, let experts do their jobs, and don't wear so many hats that you either forget to direct your movie or end up arriving at all decisions by committee.

> Keep up-to-date on advances in different cameras' capabilities and how their strengths and weaknesses would suit or hinder your creative goals. If image quality is more important than mobility, you might be better served by renting a very high-end camera instead of purchasing your own equipment. But if

you need constant access to the camera and you'll be shooting guerrilla-style, you might want to own something that you can hide in a jacket pocket.

> Always be aware of your tradeoffs among budget size, time constraints, image quality, technical expertise, creative control, product longevity, and storytelling goals. Rushing out to point-and-shoot your material is almost as bad as spending your life just talking about your movie without ever actually making it. With the accessibility of digital video and the right amount of preparation, you can strike a productive balance between the two extremes.

chapter
five

>>>*IMAGE ISN'T EVERYTHING*

Digital features, on a shoestring budget, are much cheaper than even the barest-boned film production. With the right preparation and favors, for an expenditure in the thousands of dollars, you can shoot in multiple locations with a large cast. And you can feed everybody, because you're not spending thousands of dollars on film stock, a film camera, and the gear to support it, not to mention the costs of developing film footage. So on the plus side of independent digital filmmaking is the absolute freedom to express yourself and your personal ideas, while going your own way for a comparatively minimal amount of money. On the minus side is the possible result that you go deep into debt anyway, because this idea of yours is so personal and intimate that nobody wants to see it. This is one reason why so many independent films never see the light of day, or *do* see the light of day but never make a dime. However, if this were truly a fear that gripped you, you wouldn't be thinking about shooting your own feature. Our tips concerning shooting a digital feature are followed by inspiring profiles of ordinary folks like yourself who have gone out and done exactly that.

SOME WORDS OF ADVICE ON SHOOTING

> On a film shoot, when every second that the camera rolls costs the production significant bucks, it forces everyone on the crew to be extremely careful and do their absolute best. Not that those things can't be true on a video shoot, but the fear of wasting tons of money usually makes people work hard. When it's really cheap and easy, it's easy not to pay attention.

> Shoot low contrast (for instance, under overcast skies instead of in direct sunlight) and avoid high contrast situations in order to avoid lack of detail on images.

> Have your art department get together with the camera department to make sure the colors on set don't clash for video, and that there are not too many textures in the background to avoid a strobing effect if the camera moves quickly from one position to another.

> Be aware that the color differentiation and color range is simply not as good on digital video as it is on film. On film, there are 100 steps between colors; on video, there are 50 steps between colors. Because of this, big landscape vistas, an epic feel, and bright daylight exteriors are going to be much tougher to pull off on digital video.

> Make digital acquisition part of the look of your picture, rather than always fighting a battle to pretend that it's film.

> The best post-production is good pre-production. In other words, allow the time and money to do it right the first time; no matter how painful in the moment, this is almost always cheaper and more effective than trying to fix problems in post.

> Making a movie can help your writing tremendously, especially in terms of editing your writing and finding what dialogue and scenes are truly necessary to convey the emotion at the heart of the story. But you can save yourself time and money by using staged readings, taped rehearsals, and a rigorous development process to make your shooting script as tight and well-crafted as possible before you get to the set.

> Consider whether it serves your story best to own or rent your camera. If the latter, this is a good area to stretch the budget allowance for the payoff in resolution and color range. For example, a DVCAM is only slightly more expensive to rent than a mini-DV, but it will give you several quantum leaps in image quality. So if you're willing to invest a little more money you can get a lot more production value.

> Shooting 16:9 gets you closer to the 1.85:1 width-to-height ratio of a 35-millimeter movie screen, as opposed to a 4:3 ratio that is similar to television's 1.33:1 frame. If you plan to project your video movie on a big screen someday, you can shoot in 16:9 while not putting anything terribly important at the very top or very bottom of your frame (because those areas will get cropped in a theater projection at a 1.85:1 ratio).

> The difference between "squeezed" 16:9 and "true" 16:9 is that in true 16:9 the CCD chip itself is shaped in a 16:9 frame. You can also put an anamorphic adaptor on the camera to achieve this. But if your camera came with a 4:3 CCD, then when you tell it to shoot 16:9 it will obey by taking out some CCD lines from the top and bottom. If you play back your squeezed 16:9 on a regular 4:3 television monitor, everyone will look tall and skinny. However, this works better for a film transfer than simply shooting a straight 4:3 that is framed for 1.85 in the viewfinder without telling the camera to do anything special in the recording process.[5]

> Film shows more of the frame than an NTSC monitor, so keep a TV-safe inner boundary to the frame so that you don't cut off the tops of people's heads, the person at the side of the screen, etc.

> As technology prices continue to drop and capabilities continue to expand, low-budget independent filmmakers can look forward to getting more affordable access to HD and 24P cameras. However, there comes a point where you keep waiting for the best technology at the cheapest rates, and then you never do anything. If you want to tell a story, buy or rent yourself the best digital camera you can, and go do it.

---

[5]"The Truth Is In What You See," James Tocher, *RES Magazine*, January/February 2001

SOME PEOPLE WHO HAVE GONE AND DONE IT

In his first digital feature, *Wake*, writer-director Roy Finch was trying to get as close to film as possible. Looking back on the project, he thinks that if he had used 35-millimeter the piece wouldn't have been as raw and intense. Lighting requirements, for one thing, would probably have gotten in the way of fostering an ongoing intimacy and suspension of disbelief among the characters, a group of dysfunctional brothers reunited in the house they grew up in. He would also shoot on HD if he were to go the digital route again, since the heavy compression of DV leads to the degradation of the image.

For *Wake*, they shot on a Sony DSR 500 WSP (the last letters stand for wide-screen and PAL). They chose the PAL system because it captures images at 25fps, and in a transfer to film's 24fps they would just have to slow the film down a touch. (If you shoot NTSC at 30fps, some film transfer processes actually pull out frames and lose video information, with an end product that doesn't look as good.)

In pre-production, Finch's team created digital storyboards with digital stills from the Sony PD 150. They blocked scene rehearsals, took pictures, and printed them out as a series of storyboards. They had arrived in the location (an old house in Maine) two days before shooting, but previously, they had had a week of intense rehearsals in Los Angeles, even flying out one of the principal actors from Maine. This really paid off in the building intensity of the film, which drew on the intimacy that the actors and director discovered in that week of rehearsal. Their final budget was well under $100,000, and a lot of their savings in both time and money came from the fact that Finch knows post-production extremely well and could handle a good deal of the editing and post himself.

Also, digital dailies were enormously helpful in the production. There was an assistant editor on set whose laptop had Final Cut Pro, and a little monitor. In the evenings, Finch could go up to see what they had shot that day. This feedback allowed him to see if he was missing a shot, or if something wasn't cutting together quite right. Plus, he was able to see whether he captured the performance on tape, with the benefit of distance from the heat of the moment.

After raising money privately with the help of attached name Martin Landau, who has a featured role, they had a month of pre-production. During that time, Finch met with his cinematographer to establish the aesthetic and visual style he was going for. They looked through photographs to discuss framing, focus and depth of field; they also looked at filmed versions of stage plays, since Finch's piece was almost written with the same continuous feel as a theatrical play. Because digital video doesn't do well when faced with strong contrasts in light and dark, he staged the entire film in one night, inside. This digital decision also lent itself to the play format that they were working with. They prepared their shooting schedule on Movie Magic software, and shot a lot more of the movie than made it into the final version. They made rough floor plans (lines and boxes representing room dimensions and furniture placement) of every shooting area in order to plan for lighting, blocking, and camera setups.

The shoot itself lasted seventeen days, the first two of which overlapped with the end of pre-production. There's a lot of dialogue in the movie, and they moved at an unheard-of pace of 12 and 15 pages a day (on a film set, you'd be happy to shoot five pages a day). Finch attributes this speed partly to his own rookie determination to plow forward and get it done (with this experience under his belt, he doesn't know if he would push at the same rate, next time around), partly to the nature of the script and the self-contained locations (which fostered long takes and intense, continuous performances from the actors) and partly to the flexibility of the digital camera and lighting setups. Days were about 12 hours long, from 7 a.m. to 7 p.m., keeping to a daytime shooting schedule even (although the entire story takes place at night). They gelled the windows to simulate darkness, and rented a lighting package to go with their camera.

Finch encouraged the actors to improvise on set, but found in the editing that almost none of those unscripted moments made it into the final cut — and that was just his editor taking out things that didn't fit. On the other hand, the process also afforded him some gems that made the extra footage worth it. Still, the danger of shooting endless footage is that it can take away some of the focus of crafting something, as opposed to proceeding with a certain randomness, if you're not careful.

He remembers one of the best moments on set as being a full twelve-minute take of the main character's climactic scene, and just knowing he was getting the heart of the film. "That we had nailed it, that he had nailed it, that the composition, and the hand-held quality, was exactly as I had wanted it to be in my heart." The low point on set was when an actor in a cameo role was unable to manage the poetic monologue Finch had given her. Unsuccessfully attempting to coax a usable performance out of that scene was the opposite of his best moment, as he went through the frustration of trying different things, and seeing that nothing was working. Later, they had to cut that monologue out of the film's last scenes entirely, and that actually ended up being a good thing, since the final sequence turned out to be much stronger without the monologue.

Finch used multi-track sound recording and a DAT recorder for a cleaner sound. Good sound is definitely one thing not to skimp on — if you've been to a film festival, you've seen a first feature where an inexpert sound mixer on set resulted in a kitchen breakfast conversation that sounded like a battle scene as a spatula scraped across a metal frying pan at the same decibel level as the dialogue conversation, or actors set their juice glasses down with deafening hits. Sound is also extremely expensive to fix in post, where foleying, sound mixes, and ADR studio time run hundreds of dollars an hour. If there's one crew member you want to pay (other than perhaps your director of photography), pay a professional sound mixer and give him or her the necessary equipment for the job. There's also a crew position in DV called the video technician, who tells you if there's enough information for a film transfer; meaning, is there enough digitally acquired image to work with in post. So as a director, you'll have to get used to watching performances through the monitor, and to paying someone to help you evaluate how robust your digital signal is.

That is, unless you're shooting guerrilla style, as San Franciscan David Schendel did in making his documentary *Yank Tanks*. Schendel filmed this piece — about the vibrant subculture of Cubans who own and adore American cars from the 1950s — with the Canon GL1. This camera has a fake progressive scan mode called Frame Mode. With this mode selected, the video doesn't overlap fields as it's recording, and each frame is a frame, so it's more like film. Oddly, even though all the transfer labs told Schendel not to do this, it ended up looking better after the film transfer. "Take the lab advice with a grain of salt," he says, "because their priority is to turn your transfer around as fast as possible to make the greatest profit. They've got all these rules, but most of the advances come from people who broke the rules." Schendel found a look that he liked and he stuck with it. He didn't use special lenses, but he treated the camera as a camera, and exposed video as if it had been film. By not letting the machine take over, by invading the machine instead, he got himself more interesting results.

For his documentary footage and informal interview style, Schendel would sometimes attach a clip-on lavaliere microphone to the person speaking, but half the time he used the onboard stereo microphone because he was shooting wide and getting the camera as close as he could to the subject in a controlled environment. This had the happy side effect of giving the audio a three-dimensional feeling — roosters crowing, neighbors' voices in lively Cuban neighborhoods and so on — without laying extra tracks. Admittedly, some takes were unusable because of sound problems, but that was a risk Schendel was willing to take.

To raise financing for the documentary, Schendel first went to Cuba and came back with a few hours of footage, which he then cut into a four-minute trailer of what he wanted to do. This kind of trailer can be a very useful fundraising tool, and was particularly important for Schendel because he had no track record on paper at that time. With a business plan, a treatment (a summary and project proposal) and a VHS copy of his trailer in hand, Schendel approached people for money and was able to put together enough to return to Cuba to do the real shoot. He warns that you have to be careful with whom you share your ideas with — after he approached PBS, PBS in Brooklyn coincidentally released a half-hour documentary about Cuban cars, at the same time as Schendel's film was coming out.

When he got to his final cut, he had a test screening at the Film Arts Foundation in San Francisco, giving the 80 members of his audience response questionnaires to fill out afterwards. This kind of feedback can be incredibly valuable if you want new points of view on your film. The transfer to film was done at Heavy Light Digital, which charged $28,000 for a 70-minute transfer. The other big ticket in the $150,000 budget was music licensing, because the Cuban jazz and hip-hop on the soundtrack was such an integral part of giving the film its Cuban feel. Schendel's investment paid off, though, when distributors picked up his digital documentary for theatrical release.

A guerrilla effort closer to home was completed by J. C. Calciano, whose *Coming Out: A Collection of Stories* was shot in a combination of people's homes, in a studio setting, and on the street, while Calciano used a Canon XL1, a reflector board, and a microphone to ask gay men and women about their experiences in coming out to friends and family. They shot on the streets of New York City and West Hollywood, and no one ever hassled them while they quietly shot a personal, compelling feature documentary with a tiny, unobtrusive crew.

And now, back to the story that began the first chapter of this book. With the screenplay for *Washington Heights* nearly ready for shooting, Alfredo Rodriguez de Villa began reaching out to friends and contacts in the film industry. Tom Donahue, co-owner of the post-production house Stolen Car Productions and himself a successful editor with whom Alfredo had previously worked, became involved as a producer. At a film festival where he was screening his short film *Neto's Run*, Alfredo met Joe La Morte and Gloria Herrera, who quickly became interested in finding investors for the film. At the same time, Alfredo was introduced to producers Peter Newman and Greg Johnson, whose impressive list of credits included groundbreaking independent films like *Swimming to Cambodia* and *Smoke*.

Even with this team on board, Alfredo says, finding the money was very discouraging and very difficult. "You don't know until you're on the first day of the set that you're going to actually shoot." Still, by the spring of 2001, a large portion of the financing for *Washington Heights* had fallen into place. Through a mutual acquaintance Alfredo was able to get a copy of the script to casting director Brett Goldstein. Goldstein loved the script and it was through him that veteran actors Tomas Milian, Danny Hoch and Jude Ciccolella (who, like the rest of the cast, have been seen in numerous mainstream and independent films and TV shows) were brought to the project with the agreement that they would work for deferred salaries. Once they were cast, Alfredo gave all the actors great leeway to make their characters their own in the rehearsal process, and Moss completed a final rewrite on the production draft in the week before shooting commenced, incorporating discoveries made by the actors.[6]

As they got close to the projected start date, the production money that had come into place suddenly went away, as sometimes happens. But by that point they had a project, cast, and creative team that was much more attractive than anything they'd had before, and that was much easier to sell than something theoretical. It also helped that they were telling a kind of story that wasn't being seen in the Latino market. So they were able to get a new infusion of money, and then the other financing came back.

Picture Washington Heights in New York City, a mostly Latino neighborhood above Harlem, north of 180th Street and continuing on into the

---

[6]From "The Making of Washington Heights" by Alfredo Rodriguez de Villa and Nat Moss

low 200s (currently the yuppies are found in increasing concentrations as you travel southward from 110th Street). The roads are narrow and full of pedestrians and cars; there's a lively community feeling there, and a lot of little mom-and-pop type stores. A principal setting of *Washington Heights* is one of these skinny, food-stuffed corner bodegas. The size of the digital camera and the fewer lights and crew members required made it possible for Alfredo to work in these confined spaces. If they were in a kitchen, he'd put the camera on a skateboard. When they shot in this very small bodega, they could move the camera. Shooting on film would have been a nightmare. There wasn't even room for a monitor. It was just the cinematographer, and Alfredo behind him, and the actors in the scene.

To minimize digital video's limitations in resolution and color, they used a PAL format camera, anticipating that its 25fps would make for a better transfer to film. They also shot with two cameras at once, since the low costs of tape and equipment were more than compensated for in the extra footage and editing options they had. Alfredo would absolutely shoot on digital again, remembering the freedom it provided him in *Washington Heights*. Shooting (instead of standing around and waiting for lighting setups) all day left a lot of room for improvisation, both in acting and in camera work. By shooting with a zoom lens, they could easily and quickly choose different frames for successive takes. Which meant no shot ever had to be the same, and that gave them a wide variety of editing options.

Alfredo shot *Washington Heights* in eighteen days, keeping to a six-page-a-day baseline. Company moves (packing up the crew and equipment and moving to another location) were kept to a minimum, with about 80% of the movie being shot in an area of 10 square blocks, often in adjacent buildings. If they had stayed with their original intention of shooting on film, they would have been at the whim of someone else buying into their idea and being willing to invest hundreds of thousands (if not millions) of dollars in it. But as a digital feature, they could get someone to invest in their idea for a fraction of that — for about $250,000 in the case of *Washington Heights*.

In fact, not having that high a budget can work to a filmmaker's advantage when casting actors who are members of the Screen Actors Guild. Not all good actors are in SAG, but certainly many good ones are, and as union members they are obligated to charge you fees on a set scale. They can defer these fees if you promise to pay them the proper rate once your movie starts making profits. This is a common practice on low-budget films, and it is widely known that some actors will never see their eventual payouts because the films may never go into the black. Once your budget rises over $75,000 for experimental films (or $500,000 for the modified low-budget bracket specified by SAG) the standard daily rates for your actors jump up as well. Kind of like income taxes. However, once you have a SAG waiver for a film of a specified budget, you'd better stay within that budget and those rules for how actors are treated, or face steep penalties in monetary fines, cast loyalty, and production slowdowns.

THE WRAP

> Shooting your feature, especially your first feature, on digital video can open up flexibility, experimentation, and creative freedom on set without all the pressures of a film budget riding on your every decision.

> Low-budget filmmaking carries its own kind of pressures, though, sometimes limiting options such as re-shoots and extended shooting schedules. For this reason, it's critical to give yourself the benefit of exhaustive pre-production, which includes polishing and paring down the script so that you don't waste time and money shooting scenes where the writing doesn't work.

> The biggest time- and money-saver you'll have is knowing what you want beforehand, and getting it right during production, rather than trying to fix it in post.

Remember that once you include time spent in post-production and trying to get the movie seen, you have to live through your script for years, and so you have to really find a script that you are very passionate about. By Alfredo's reckoning, having spent two years writing the script and raising money, and having gotten through the exhausting battle of a month-long physical production, as shooting finished, they were really less than halfway through their journey. They then faced the next step: editing.

PART II
MAKING THE CUT

chapter
six

>>>*LIGHT MY FIREWIRE*

Here are parts two and three of the fantasy: having shot a brilliant movie for $50 using your own DV camera, you then plug the camera into your computer and take a couple of months to edit the digital footage into a finished motion picture. Then, with your freshly completed film dubbed onto videotape, you become recognized, rich, and famous.

Jaded summary aside, there is a valid approach underlying this process, and things not too far from this have actually happened. The key is in understanding how much more than you expect goes into the steps mentioned above. You can edit digital footage on several different scales: at home on your own computer; via the hired services of a professional editor; or in a full-scale post-production house.

EDITING ON YOUR OWN COMPUTER

This computer might be one that belongs to you, or one that you can use through your relationship with a school, a business, a cable access station, or a caring friend. The more electronic accessories and tools you can get for free, the better, of course. But if you need to acquire non-free stuff, there's a lot to be said for renting versus purchasing, given the high costs and rapid obsolescence of most digital gadgets, and the access to technical advice, repair service, and equipment replacement available through a good rental company (because something could always go wrong). Don't buy any more equipment than you need, unless you want to become a post-production house.

You arrive on day one of editing, with limited time and a movie to make. You have a box full of the DV tapes from your shoot. You are immediately faced with one of the most tedious and painful parts of the filmmaking process: logging your footage. Even assuming that you are looking at time-coded video dailies, you as a director and editor have to watch each shot in real time to find out which takes worked technically, which takes you prefer artistically, and whether any coverage (*vis à vis* camera angles, story, continuity) is missing. You can try to entertain yourself during this lengthy process by keeping a record of funny outtakes. Meanwhile, you'll be making exhaustive notes — the more the better — on what footage you want to start editing with. Because, unless you own or rent multiple hard drives, it's going to be very cumbersome for you to capture every camera take onto your computer.

"Capturing" is the process of importing from your DV tape into your computer's memory via an IEEE1394 connector like a FireWire or an i.Link. In addition to eating up memory storage space, capturing happens in real time — in other words, a take that lasts two minutes will take two minutes to import into your hard drive. The longer the take, the greater the chance that a glitch in the capture will make the imported footage unusable. A good rule of thumb is to limit your captures to four- or five-minute chunks at the longest. And it may seem to save time if you ignore a glitch or two in the footage when you're just starting out; you'll say to yourself, *Well, this is just a rough cut, I can always re-capture that glitchy take later. For now I don't mind if a brilliant white streak flashes through the frame, or if for a split second my actor looks like he's having a stroke. I just want to keep moving.* The problem is that you may end up using a glitchy take in a beautifully edited sequence, and you will pay for this in frustration and re-doing the edit down the road. Doing it right the first time is the best time-saver there is.

That also applies to what you create while shooting on set, but we'll keep this discussion to what can be usefully mulled over in the edit bay. What you *can* do at this point is be strategic in your choices of which takes to use and how to approach editing them. If your computer system is slow because of memory or operating speed, making a detailed, thorough game plan before you sit down can save you hours of fiddling around (this is especially important if you don't have unlimited access to the editing system).

Massive amounts of memory are necessary to edit a film and have some room left over for the computer itself to operate at something faster than a crawl. Non-compressed digital component would take about a gigabyte of memory per minute. At low resolution — strictly for editing purposes — you can squeeze about 30 minutes of footage into a gigabyte of hard-drive space. Using a non-linear editing program (such as Final Cut Pro or Adobe Premiere — the former is generally preferred) you then cut shots together. You also can add plug-in programs to expand the range of basic transitions, filters, etc.

As you're putting together the flow and rhythm of your visual story, you're also sound editing, and incorporating temporary music tracks, voice over, foleys, and other temporary audio effects. Music and sound effects are added to video by recording them to computer files and then adding those portions of data to the audio line of your movie. Remember to acquire the legal rights to use the music publicly. If you have lower-end visual effects, AfterEffects and similar programs allow you to preview all your visual effects, including compositing, so that you can make well-informed decisions before either finalizing your own effects or spending more money on post-production elsewhere.

Finally, the edited video files are "rendered" (made into a single file using the many clips, transitions, and so on). If this is as far as you're taking the process, your rendered file is transferred from the computer's hard drive to a digital or analog tape, a DVD, or streaming video to show on the Internet.

For people who are considering a more professional finish and a film transfer, audio sweetening by a technician in a studio can adjust the balance and blend of your sound mix. Even if you don't have a penny to spare for this costly process (in the ballpark of $200 an hour), at the very least, you can talk to audio specialists (under the guise of getting their estimate for working on your project) for free, and glean valuable tips and information from them in the process. With the sound mix laid back onto a Digital Beta output, you can color time (make the lighting and looks match with whatever you wish) your movie either at an outside facility or with the tools in the Final Cut Pro package. When you do your video color timing, generally you try to reduce contrast and increase color saturation. Then, the transfer to film converts the digital image into a more filmic product that can be recorded onto a film negative, after which you go through the usual process of striking prints.

Basic principles apply even if you've previously edited on computer systems:

> Plan ahead. Being a creative person doesn't mean you get to be flaky. Keep (and label) your receipts from the editing process — lunches, parking, cell phone calls, office supplies, etc. You may be able to deduct these expenses on your tax return, and you want to be able to answer to an audit if your "self-employed artist" itemizations raise a red flag with the IRS.

> Allow for your own learning curve and give yourself time, patience, and flexibility. Things inevitably take longer than you want or expect them to. Count on this, and allow as much time for your edit as you can. Having some buffer time in your schedule also will allow you to have more patience with yourself, delay burnout, and allow for some experimentation in the editing choices you make.

> As you make different versions and sequences, back up your files to external disks. And keep records of footage logs and the differences between different edit versions. It's time consuming, but not as time-consuming as not having any records when you need them.

> Avoid the most common pitfall of new digital filmmakers: namely, not having all the material you need when you get to the editing room. The economics of a no-budget film prohibit you from doing reshoots, so you're going to be stuck with the material that you've shot. Then again, if you're shooting with your own digital camera, you may have some flexibility to solve problems in the editing room. On Michael Mayer's short *The Date*, the two main characters get back to the guy's apartment after dinner, he says he's going to slip into something more comfortable, and the girl stares at the ceiling for a long time while waiting for him. In the script it's very funny, but the editor came on board after shooting was completed, and found that there was nothing in the footage that could show the girl's POV of the ceiling and make the comic moment work. At this discovery, the director grabbed the camera, adjusted the lighting, grabbed half a dozen takes of the cottage cheese ceiling of the editing suite, and boom, they had the shot they needed.

> Step back from the project from time to time to get perspective. Know your own work rhythms, and respect the times that you're on a roll, as well as the times when you're too tired or distracted to really be productive. Sometimes the best thing you can do for the project is come back fresh the next day.

> Test the movie with an *audience*, even if it's a short. Find out what plays, what's too long, and what's missing. Ask for feedback, but use it selectively. As we've said, you're a fool not to listen to anyone else's ideas; you're also a fool to listen to *everyone* else's ideas. Many projects have stalled because a filmmaker was too wrapped up in his or her own unalterable opinions about what worked and didn't, and probably even more have stalled because a filmmaker tried to incorporate too many suggestions from well-meaning, intelligent people.

> Your own vision and voice are what give your project life, integrity, and unique appeal, so choose viewers carefully before you show your work to them, especially if you're in an early stage.

Roy Finch edited his DV feature *Wake* on Final Cut Pro on the Macintosh G4. All the audio was done on ProTools HD, which is a high-end software application. Finch's background is in post-production, so this was an aspect of the film he was already very comfortable with. His post team had three Macintosh systems running, more or less simultaneously. One would handle most of the graphics, such as the opening titles, end credits, and some digitally "aged" photographs that showed the film's characters as young boys, all done on Photoshop. The second system was primarily a ProTools system, so that was handling all the audio, including music editing and dialogue editing. Then they had a third system, which was the main system, doing Final Cut editing (they bought some new computers for these purposes, with credit cards).

Because of the technology, Finch and his editors never had to leave their loft. They could have done their post anywhere, in a mountain cabin or in Bangor, Maine. They had a person on each computer, each doing his own job. Finch edited only in the way that a director edits, and he gives a lot of credit for the look and effectiveness of the film to the expertise of their editor Gus Carpenter, a longtime professional whom Finch had called in as a favor, having met the editor while working for Zoetrope Films. Finch worked out a compensation deal that included a small per diem, room and board, and profit-sharing in the finished movie, as well as an understood commitment to hire this editor again when the next film came together.

Finch was assisting in so many parts of the post-production — including sound design and music composition — that "I literally hit a wall where I couldn't create anymore, couldn't work. Because you need to be able to stand back and see what the *film* looks like, but when you're sound designing, you're thinking, how does that straw sound when you sip from it — the minutiae are so intense that you lose sight of the big picture." For him, the worst aspect was having no money and being overworked while doing too many jobs at once. But the best part was enjoying the editing and learning a great deal from his veteran editor, sometimes playing with a scene for hours and coming up with some idea that the editor could re-invent into the film.

HIRING A SPECIALIST

When do you hire an editor? Before you shoot. The reason is that the editor is assembling the footage you shot the day before. He or she can call you on set and tell you *I'm missing a shot here, I need another piece, there's a problem with performance or sound or photography* — all before the set is taken down. If no one is carefully reviewing the footage as you shoot, it's much more difficult to find that out later and do re-shoots as opposed to having a set and crew there to just grab something. A lot of smaller shoots can't afford to hire the editor right away because they can only look as far as shooting, and then they start to look at all the footage, and then they hire an editor.

However, says editor John Coniglio, "Anyone serious about trying to get distribution hires an editor before the shoot, so that the editor is working a day behind camera." This allows for communication between the editor and the director at all times. In this scenario, when you're done shooting, a couple days later you'll have an assembly, as opposed to having to wait a few months more.

The cost of an editor depends on the budget. If you're shooting a feature, it's a negotiated thing based on what has already been budgeted up-front. On a short film, you sometimes have more leeway; editors who want to keep honing their craft may consider a short-term freebie so that they can use the completed footage on their own reels.

What interests editors is the quality of the script, and the question of what looks most likely to be a project that will be completed. Here is where the professionalism of your package and self-presentation comes into play. If you have a well-written script, with name actors attached, and you and your producers have your feet on the ground with a realistic attitude and proven experience, then an editor will know that your movie is going to get completed. (As opposed to a piece where it's not clear whether an audience would ever go see it, whether the production team knows what it's doing, and whether a distributor is likely to buy that project.)

Like any craft, editing takes time and talent to develop. The key is practice — the longer an editor has been doing it, the better he or she has gotten at it. Over years of experience, editors learn how to handle films, how to collaborate with directors, and how to bring out the emotion or humor in a scene. If you're hiring an editor, look at the material the person has cut, look at the resume, and determine how well you can get along with this individual. You're going to be spending a lot of time together, and working very closely — are you going to be arguing all the time, or are you going to be able to get the work done in a timely fashion? Any editor who's been doing it for a while can probably do a good job editing your feature or short. The critical difference is, which ones can you get along with and have a good time working with? That's what you should look for when you sit down in a meeting with a prospective editor: are both of you really enjoying yourselves, and can you have a productive and satisfying creative relationship.

Some editors come equipped with their own software and systems; others will look to you to put up the cost of either renting or providing facilities. Either way, the first part of the editor's job is to look at all the footage and be able to include any details seen in logging. After logging and digitizing all the material to be edited, the editor then starts work with the director (and sometimes the producer as well, if the director and producer are not the same person) to get the ball rolling on a chosen path. The director will visit to suggest tweaks, see new rough cuts, and review cuts that have been tweaked. Gradually this progresses to finessing the narrative and how effectively scenes convey it.

USING A PROFESSIONAL POST-PRODUCTION FACILITY

For *Washington Heights*, post-production (most of which was completed at a production company named Stolen Car) took nine months. By the time a rough cut had been assembled in the fall of 2001, director Alfredo Rodriguez de Villa had streamlined the 106-page shooting script down to 92 minutes. He showed this in several rounds of private screenings to small test audiences of friends, acquaintances in the film industry and total outsiders who knew nothing about the movie. Going back to the cutting room a few months later, Alfredo took another 14 minutes out of the film while keeping the essential story intact. The result is a lean, fast-paced story. When the film was accepted into the Tribeca Film Festival in April, Alfredo launched into an intense month-long work schedule to finish the movie. He completed his color correction and sound mix in the final days of April and early May leading into the festival. Work was completed literally at 10 p.m. the night before the first Tribeca screening, the film's world premiere.[7]

During the nine-month editing process, three different editors worked on the film. The first and main editor was also Alfredo's co-producer, Tom Donahue. Following that, significant restructuring was done by Jaime Valdueza, who filled two walls with scene-by-scene index cards to see what was working. Where cuts weren't working, they would make decisions to lose certain shots, trim the tails of others and so on, until, pictorially, the movie was perfect, but the story needed to get in shape. Due to the other commitments of the first editors, at this point Alfredo hired editor John Coniglio, who brought a strong understanding of narrative and pacing to the final cut.

The most satisfying part of the process for Alfredo was finding the natural moments of the story that were not written into the script. In the story, after the main character's girlfriend leaves him there's a music cue, then the camera stops and watches the neighborhood, and you have a moment to drink it in and let the life come back into the movie. "That was not in the script," Alfredo says. "It was just that the rhythm felt nice. That was Jaime's call, and I went back to my material and

---

[7]From "The Making of Washington Heights" by Alfredo Rodriguez de Villa and Nat Moss

found footage that I had already shot of the neighborhood, and then I talked to my composer about a cue that could express that moment."

Sound work and the film blowup cost $150,000. Alfredo was able to get Avid Film Composer facilities for free because of his work in commercial production and because co-producer Tom Donahue owns an Avid. But even if they had cut the movie in Final Cut Pro, they could have produced the editing decision list for the online; no one cares how the editors get to the EDL, so long as it's there. With the EDL list and a cut on Beta just as a time-code reference, they went to an online machine called Smoke (from the ProLogic software system). Original DV footage got loaded into the Smoke machine at a one-to-one data rate, without compression. Then the machine conformed the footage to the EDL based on the time-codes, and reassembled the film at high resolution. There's a 3% error margin in this process, so it's necessary to check against the Beta output from the Avid to make sure that everything is exactly as you want it.

Then came the hardest and most creative part, color correcting, on the same machine. For instance, Alfredo spent a lot of time working on the windows in various shots. Video's high contrast has a tendency to blow out the light seen from inside windows, so Alfredo cut mattes around problematic windows in order to lower the contrast levels or make a midday scene look like it had been shot at the end of the day. Instead of reading the light as golden, if you tell the machine to read that light as blue, lo and behold, it's nighttime.

For example, in the *Washington Heights* script there were supposed to be several different glimpses of the main character Carlos, who is a comic book artist, drawing different things. But in the screenings, they found that people didn't care about these sequences after seeing him draw for the first time. After taking out some of that footage, though, they created a montage of a breakthrough the character has at the drawing board following a crazy period in his personal life. Originally, that footage at the drawing board was shot in Act 1 in

Carlos's girlfriend's apartment, but after color timing them to look like the other scenes after Carlos moves into his father's apartment in Act 2, Alfredo was able to make them match visually, so that they worked dramatically.

Once color correction was done, Alfredo got a DigiBeta master, which he sent to Swiss Effects for a film transfer. *Washington Heights* was shot on the Canon XL1, but just the way the camera is made, the images may actually be a little out of focus, so 90% of the movie was likely to be *slightly* out of focus. To compensate for this, the Swiss Effects engineers reduced the image on the negative to make it a 1.85:1 aspect ratio. With 1.85, there's less information in the image, so the image is a little bit reduced, with a little less detail, and when projected on film, it's sharp and beautiful (even though it was shot on digital video).

THE WRAP

> Get an editor to come on board before you start shooting. Whether you pay this editor or call in a mighty favor, he or she can help you evaluate whether your footage, day by day, is cutting together and serving your storytelling goals.

> Having an editor working a day behind camera is important because the worst thing you can do to yourself is step into the editing room without all the footage you need, whether it's because of poor performances, technical problems, or missing coverage.

> Especially if you are going to edit your movie yourself, allow for plenty of time, plan ahead, and keep meticulous records of everything from time-coded shots to parking receipts. You'll thank yourself later.

> In order to preserve your individual vision, ask for help when you need it, step away for perspective, test your material with an audience, and remember the instincts and goals that got you excited about the project to begin with.

Professional editors agree that while they used to be in a very narrow-ly restricted trade of people with experience on, and access to, flatbeds and Movieolas, computer technology and nonlinear systems now allow everyone to try his or her hand at editing. But like any other craft, expertise in the field requires time and talent to develop, and while digital video facilitates doing it all yourself, make sure that the editing of your product is going to be as compelling, skillful, and effec-tive as it can be. In other words, don't pat yourself on the back for simply being able to *complete* the edit, without thinking about whether it's *good*. Still, whether you're teaching yourself on your home computer, hiring an outside editor to collaborate with, or taking your project to a full-service production house, digital editing makes it easier than ever before to serve the vision of the story you want to tell.

chapter
seven

>>>THE MOUSE THAT ROARED

Digital effects have provided an entirely separate engine for the revolution. While green-screens and CGI are out of the budget range of most independent filmmakers, more creative options are available than ever before to the average low-budget filmmaker working on his or her own computer. Titling, animation, image alteration, and special effects are now available to consumers through off-the-shelf software like AfterEffects and Animation Master. As with cinematography, editing, and sound, however, there is always a tradeoff of money for expertise in hiring a specialist rather than learning to do it yourself.

Does your digital movie really need effects? Consider how integral they are to the story. If they're really crucial, it might be worth the money to make them look really good. If they're not, make sure you are being true to the story you want to tell and the professionalism with which you are able to present it. For new filmmakers, sometimes it's worth holding back your grand visual effects plans on an early piece. After doing a terrific job on a simpler story, you can use that piece of work to convince more people to help you (meaning, give you money) to get visual effects and a more elaborate production the next time around, at which point you'll have experience and a learning curve already taken care of.

In the interest of empowering you with a perspective on the digital effects world at large, we will address the following: *some of the really cool stuff that's out there, some of the more practical stuff that's out there, viewpoints from the visual effects industry*, and the question of *whether you yourself could be a digital artist someday*. Ultimately, all these tools serve one thing: the story. And if the story isn't there, all the effects in the world won't make people sit down and watch.

SOME OF THE REALLY COOL STUFF THAT'S OUT THERE

One of the most common effects you see in movies these days is com-positing, which digitally blends different elements (green-screen back-ground, live action, virtual lighting, digitally generated characters, miniatures, animation and so on) into a seamless whole. For example, digital artist Eric Weinschenk told us about his work on the visual effects for *Star Trek: Nemesis*. In that movie, there's a fight in the Jeffries tubes between Commander Riker and a bad guy called the Viceroy; at the end of the struggle, the Viceroy falls down the shaft to his death. Weinschenk started work on the sequence once he was given plates, or live-action shots, from the green-screen soundstage.

In this film footage, the actor playing the Viceroy hangs down from a wire, slowly falling towards the green-screen, waving his hands and legs. The lights on the sides of the tunnel were computer-generated later, but they also had a real light right next to the Viceroy to represent lights flashing over his body as he fell past the sides of the shaft. Because these uneven practical lights made him blend into the green-screen, his body had to be rotoscoped (meaning that they drew a line around him to tell the computer where the key image ended and the background began) by hand, and roto-ed again with a different tool to account for the blurriness of him waving his hands.

After that, the 3-D department gave Weinschenk a match move to use for the background of the Jeffries tube shaft, and another match for the movement of the lights. He used a plug-in from Flint (the rest was done in Nuke proprietary software) to add a lens flare over the whole shot. This made viewers think that there was an actual camera lens responding to an actual brilliant light at the bottom of this tunnel in the spaceship. Double-printing the shot allowed Weinschenk to take every frame and double it, so that this half-second long moment, which previously used 36 frames, now lasted 72 frames in a stuttery effect to heighten the moment. The finished product is a very convincing shot of the Viceroy falling past flashing instrument panels before disappearing into a bril-liant light at the bottom of a high-tech abyss.

Once digital artists have a complete set of instructions for the computer, the computer renders the footage and executes all the things it's been told to do — just as Adobe Premiere has to render clips before you can preview them on your Macintosh screen at home. Up until that point, artists are working with fairly low resolution, minimizing their operating memory requirements by only looking at every five, 10, or 20 frames. Because rendering is such a time- and memory-intensive process, a sub-industry of render farms will take jobs and turn them around quickly. At big effects houses like Digital Domain, every computer's memory is linked into the rendering server, so that when one computer is idle it's helping to render other work.

Rendered files are then outputted to film so that dailies can be screened by post supervisors, visual effects supervisors, producers and directors, who either give approval or ask for further creative refinements — make the Jeffries tube darker but not super-dark, make the Viceroy more blue, change how fast he falls, do something differently in marrying the foreground to the 3-D background — and the digital artist's job is to make the shot believable in accordance with client's wishes.

One pitfall of this flexibility in the review process is a tendency unofficially known as "pixel-f**king," in other words the desire to manipulate every little thing and pick at it like a scab. Sometimes people want to manipulate things, even though they're beautiful to begin with. Weinschenk worked on a shot in Gattaca where Uma Thurman's hand looked bigger than expected, sitting next to Ethan Hawke's while they were playing with each other's fingers on a date. Weinschenk was asked to use a morphing program (warping programs like Elastic Reality and Matador create some of those morphing effects we all know and enjoy) to reduce the size of Uma's hand by a third so that it looked suitably dainty. Then there are the people who'll say they'll just paint things out in post, and it takes someone a month to digitally erase Tom Cruise's safety wires from a shot of him climbing up a sheer cliff face. A longer-sighted view of the costs and time involved would dictate that it actually makes more sense to just shoot certain things a different way to begin with; this is something to keep in mind when you're budgeting your own digital shoot.

Many advances in digital effects have come out of the needs of certain stories, which drive new technologies to accommodate them. Director Peter Jackson wanted to show the battles of *The Lord of the Rings* in all their scale and complexity, but previous movies had relied on either costly live extras or digital armies and crowds that could only behave like uniform, two-dimensional paper cutouts. So Jackson went to computer programmer Stephen Regelous, and Regelous created Massive, a special effects software program that digitally generates characters, or agents, who have the ability to make individual decisions. Digital agents choose from a repertoire of subtle motions and reactions, with thousands of brain nodes that use fuzzy logic rather than yes-no, on-off decisions. Stunt actors' movements were then recorded in the studio to enable the agents to wield weapons realistically, duck to avoid a sword, charge an enemy and fall off of tower walls. Put fifty thousand of these digital agents on a battlefield together, and suddenly you no longer have a thick crowd of lock-stepped puppets. Instead, you have what looks like a living, breathing army of angry Orcs, rattling spears, choosing their responses to each other and moving in realistic, individual ways that are governed by each digital character's brain. This flocking technology, when composited with live action, miniatures and CG effects to add details such as torchlight, smoke plumes, and splashes of water, allowed Jackson to fly 3-D camera moves through the clashing armies, and resulted in the spectacular battle sequences of *The Fellowship of the Ring, The Two Towers,* and *The Return of the King.*[8]

Another digitally based technology featured in those films was motion capture, which is how the visual effects team at Weta brought the ground-breaking character Gollum to life. We realize that even basic motion capture services, in the ballpark of $12,000 a day, might be beyond the budget for what you have in mind. But just as someone opening up a corner coffee stand ought to be aware of how they run Starbucks, you ought to know what's out there, and how these digital tools apply to the evolution of storytelling in which you are partaking.

---

[8] *Wired* magazine, December 19, 2002

Say you want to investigate how motion capture is done. At the Jim Henson Creature Shop in the industrial area surrounding the Burbank Airport, you are greeted in the first demo area by Mr. Tinkles (the Persian cat villain from *Cats and Dogs*) on a computer screen, making snappy rejoinders at you and interactively working the room. Mr. Tinkles is voiced by a puppeteer using the proprietary Henson Digital Performance System, which interfaces with Maya software to control the image on the screen via the twitching fingers and wrists of the puppeteer, whose right and left hands are surrounded by a cyborg-looking glove and joystick apparatus, respectively. Every finger flick and squeeze corresponds to an isolated movement in the digital face: dilating pupils, a raised eyebrow, a sneering lip, a toss of the head. Coupled with the live delivery from the puppeteer (who is also an actor and improv comic), this results in an instantly animated, reactive performance that can be directed on set, and married to a physical animatronic device like, for instance, a cat. This way you don't have a cat puppet team doing one thing for the camera during shooting, and a separate CGI team creating a new performance for the cat's digitally superimposed face months later.

The talking-head aspect of the technology is particularly useful in interactive gaming, where Henson services might be used to put real-istic faces on character dialogue. But why stop there? In collaboration with the Xtrackrz motion-capture experts, they can give you the rest of the body as well. You proceed down the hall to a kind of airlock outside their motion-capture stage, where animated characters survey you from a TV screen set high on the wall. An elfin woman in an orange dominatrix bikini strolls back and forth, chatting up the guys (again, this is a puppeteer improvising lines while watching you through a hidden camera) while a large, friendly green troll galumphs around behind her, scratching his head. Then you get to step inside the studio, where you see the two suit performers behind the elf-woman and the troll dancing to Pat Benatar's "Heartbreaker" across a wide, empty floor lit by a ceiling-hung ring of red lights (to accommodate camera settings) while their corresponding animated creatures dance along in perfect sync on the TV monitors ringing the room. The mo-cap (motion capture) artists are wearing what look like stretchy jumpsuits overlaid with black fabric rigging. Round sensors about the size of gumballs, covered with the same highly reflective 3M material used in stop signs and running sneakers, sit on the rigging at their heads, hands, feet, and joints, as well as along their limbs and torsos.

Picture a connect-the-dots stick figure; that's what these sensors convey to the long, curved bank of computer monitors facing the stage floor, manned by pale, earnest young men with the look of late-night Playstation junkies about them. The puppeteers have their own monitors and computers, and the same cyborg gloves and joysticks to add the facial expressions to the body movements that the woman and man in the suits are providing. Theoretically, you as the director could be in there giving live direction and feedback to both the mo-cap artists and the voice-talent puppeteers. This kind of motion capture is heavily used in interactive games. For Madden Football on Playstation, all those football players started out as sensor-balled men throwing passes, hurling tackles, and doing victory shimmies in these motion capture suits. Generally, the actors were grouped into three different sizes of men — small, medium, and large — and the animators took it from there to bring you Brett Favre's face, and so on.

SOME OF THE MORE PRACTICAL STUFF THAT'S OUT THERE

Even if your digital movie is not on the scale of the projects discussed above, there are concrete ways that all this new technology can benefit you. Some of the more accessible and practical effects available are the processes whereby your digital master is given the appearance of film through manipulation in color correction and frame-like motion. At the facilities operated by The Orphanage (founded by ex-ILM innovators Stu Maschwitz, Scott Stewart, and Jonathan Rothbart), your digital footage goes through a frame-conversion process that changes it from NTSC 30fps, or from PAL 25fps, to a filmic 24fps. The company's software, Magic Bullet, also allows you to remove video artifacts (glitchy-looking DV giveaways) and tweak the levels of grain, color contrast, and pixellation, while offering various "looks" to mimic specific film lighting schemes. In short, here is a tool that lets you pretend you shot the stuff on film, even though you didn't.

Unavoidably, this is going to add to your post-production costs, especially if you take it to a facility such as Filmlook, where their engineers do the entire process for you. A 100-minute digital film, at an hour of session time per 10 minutes of film, might take a day and a half to go through Filmlook. But once you're at Filmlook, you do get to feel like a really cool director while sitting in one of their darkened session rooms on a black leather couch with a flower arrangement and a bowl of free snacks gracing the end tables (they actually prefer it if you're there to supervise and give feedback and direction on the colorist's choices). As you lounge and call out orders to the helpful technician, you look straight at his console, similar to a computer edit bay and tastefully illuminated by overhead mini-track lighting, and the small flat screen on the wall facing him. With a touch of a Star Trek-looking button, he changes the amount of grain in your digital original to look more and more like a grainy film. Where there was a clean, sterile flatness before, at the highest grain setting it looks almost like there's a constant, even motion of tiny particles over the image. Usually, they opt for a medium-grain setting, and at the same time they correct the color of the image to look richer, deeper, and less harshly lit. Then there's the frame-rate adjustment, which can take the 30fps of NTSC digital video and make it look like it was shot at 24fps.

Say you start with a digital original that shows a corporate fellow talking by a day-lit window while the camera dollies closer in a smooth, gliding movement. In the video version, this looks like an infomercial: white light pouring into a flat, shallow room, the corporate guy looks like he's under fluorescents, the camera move is so arbitrary you can almost feel the studio cameraman pushing that big rolling setup while wearing headphones and a tool-belt. Once the Filmlook adjustments happen — and you can watch these snippets over and over — with instant modifications every time (this is why you can easily spend an hour working on 10 minutes of edited footage, especially if there are fast cuts and different looks involved) — all of a sudden the corporate guy looks kindly and warm, lit by soft yellow sunshine drifting in from the window (you subliminally get the impression of a bigger room, with perceptibly different air currents and acoustics, because of the increased graininess of the image) as the frame slowly brings you closer to him. It's almost like the camera move went into slow motion. Not because it actually took any longer to get to the final frame, but because video takes you from point A to point B in a fluid movement at 30fps, and film has the effect of taking tiny gradual "steps" from one spot to another. Conversely, changing the look to 24fps can make a handheld digital camera move look jumpy because of this "steppy"-ness, and as a result you might choose to go with a higher fps to smooth out the move, sacrificing a little bit of the lighting and color look for the more important adjustment in image motion for that particular shot.

And that's just the beginning of the tweaking. For more money, but a wider range of results, you can combine the Filmlook process with the color correction capabilities of their "da Vinci 2K" suite. Filmlook founder Robert Faber describes the color correction of the da Vinci, compared to Filmlook, as "a Saturn V rocket next to fireworks." And truly, the da Vinci setup is impressive. It's kind of like a small war room from an action-adventure movie, except for the comfy black leather couch and bowl of snacks behind the consoles. As the technician touches controls, the color of a woman's shirt magically changes from blue to purple to orange without affecting anything else in the frame; the surrounding color bleeds away to create a bleach bypass look similar to that in *The Matrix*, and then color seeps back in a tinge at a time; another control adds a filter effect that makes it look like the scene was shot with a ProMist filter (which adds a slight dreaminess to outlines without taking anything out of focus), even though it wasn't; more touches on the panel, and this ProMist filter effect dials back tiny notches to create the effect of a 3/4 ProMist, a 5/8 ProMist, a 5/16 ProMist, and so on. It's pretty cool. And it's all geared to create the maximum flexibility and range to give a client exactly the look he or she wants.

Marrying the da Vinci to another outside hardware setup is nothing unusual, says Faber, since the da Vinci system is typically used in post processes that involve numerous interconnected and interfacing technologies. They're able to control the Filmlook system through the da Vinci setup, as if the Filmlook manipulations were just one more option in the da Vinci tools. What they do with gamma, or grayscale, they've imported into the custom curves feature of da Vinci; and they bring their thirteen-plus years of experience in making video look like film to the da Vinci process. Now that 24P and HD are becoming more common, they have set up da Vinci to handle both (this includes an HD monitor that Faber calls "the Lexus" because it cost the same as one).

Faber has seen a rising popularity in the DV formats, and works on more and more material acquired that way. Unfortunately, he's also seen less experience from people using those formats — people who have jumped into the picture-making world without the benefit of experience in adjusting equipment, controlling lighting exposure, and dealing with all the aspects of production, which really haven't changed. He warns that when some people just pick up the camera and point and shoot and don't believe that they have to learn any of the technical details, the results can be disappointing.

To avoid that kind of disappointment, work with an experienced cinematographer, and make sure that he or she is on hand for color correction and other steps of your digital post. Aside from offering their own expertise in those processes, cinematographers will help you maintain the quality of the image so that what the audience sees is representative of the cinematographer's work, input, and intention.

VIEWPOINTS FROM THE VISUAL EFFECTS INDUSTRY

Meanwhile, two things have changed in the visual effects industry: the paintbrush being used, and the speed expected in using it. Two things haven't changed: audience expectations that continually spiral upward, and producer/studio expectations that more and more can be done for less and less money just because computers are involved.

From a technological standpoint, the techniques become more advanced at a faster rate each year. Changes that took years to advance in the 1970s and 1980s now happen in the course of months, and the slope of change is continuing to get steeper.

The industry is cyclical, so there are periods where there's a lot of work to go around, and the large companies get fat with projects and over-head, allowing people to break off to start and grow smaller compa-nies, and anyone who has a skill-set to create computer imagery is working. Then there comes a dry spell, the smaller companies dissolve and the talented artists go back to work for the better big companies. The smaller companies who were smart (keeping overhead in check, money in reserve, and an efficient production pipeline), lean, and tal-ented remain intact. The big companies who weren't smart and did not have deep pockets fall. And the computer operators go without work. It becomes the survival of the fittest and most talented.

The biggest challenge these days, financially speaking, is for compa-nies to underbid the competition enough to get the work, but still turn a profit. And finding talented artists is always difficult in terms of what the project will afford versus what the project needs. Also, because of the dropping costs of hardware and software, everyone thinks he or she can be a digital artist, and the average citizen working out of her garage can bid at the fraction of the cost of a studio. In addition, there's the possibility of digital work (especially animation and post) being outsourced to foreign countries where people with technical skills are paid much less than they are in the United States.

Some people can make the current climate work for them, though. According to Volker Engel, who won an Oscar in Visual Effects for *Independence Day*, a small, tightly knit production crew was key to the speed and cost-effectiveness with which he and his team were able to complete the action-adventure *Coronado*. They spent half a year in pre-production, and worked up 45 minutes of previsualization (com-puter-generated images that are like animated storyboards, including camera moves and rough effects). Volker was co-writer, producer, and

VFX supervisor, working directly with 12 in-house artists at his compa-ny Uncharted Territory, rather than spending time and money going back and forth with separate production entities. For example, the animators could go straight to the director and ask if they could do two separate shots on a bridge sequence instead of a 180-degree cam-era move. The director agreed on the spot, instantly saving the pro-duction $20,000. The project benefited enormously from complete creative control, lots of preparation, and the right tools — the same things that benefit filmmakers at any budget level.

Alex MacDowell was the production designer for Steven Spielberg's futuristic *Minority Report,* and also says previsualization has become an integral step of art department pre-production. He first used the tool in *Fight Club,* where, for instance, they wanted to establish the skyline of the background buildings that would be revealed by the collapsing buildings at the film's close. Previsualization is used in planning sets, lighting schemes, and backdrops, all working in 3-D. These comput-er plans can then be transformed into physical models; MacDowell says that *Minority Report* would have been impossible to do any other way. Previsualization is also good for seeing the story when there is no set and you have to ask a crew to coordinate a complex sequence in front of an empty bluescreen.

Visual effects are alive and well on television, too. But in the world of television, there's less money and less time to get the job done. Television will have a couple of days or, perhaps, a week to turn around shots, where film usually has months or sometimes years. But if you're shooting 1920 x 1080 HD and 24P, you can't get away with an "adequate" compositing job on TV, because if someone is watch-ing a high-definition monitor, he or she can pick up the outlines and flickers that would have been hidden on a 720-line screen. Budgets now are saying everyone has to deliver HD, but no one has decided what flavor (there are several resolution- and interlace-differing variations of the format that all qualify as HD), and no one has allotted more time or money for that.

However, 24P can be useful for onscreen video playbacks. If you're shooting on film and you point the camera at a television monitor or a computer screen that has not been adjusted to match film's 24fps, you get a weird fuzzy line scrolling through the TV or computer screen. But you can point your 24fps film camera at a TV monitor that is playing back a 24fps video, and everything looks just fine. This can save time and money that would otherwise go to green-screen compositing to insert the contents of that TV screen. 24P also can create problems, though. According to Star Trek visual effects producer Dan Curry, alien prosthetics looked obviously fake on 24P, due to HD's precise capture of the image. In contrast, film acts like a Dutch Master's painting, harmonizing the light with shades and hints that the eye naturally blends together, so for their purposes, film made the 24th century a little more palatable.

COULD YOU BE A DIGITAL ARTIST?

How does one get into this industry? The motion-capture artists working with Xtrackrz and the Jim Henson Creature Shop came from dance, acting, and pantomime backgrounds, and had transitioned naturally into suit work from previous gigs. The team of producers and computer animators surrounding them had come from a variety of backgrounds including jet engineering, art school, film production, and restaurant ownership ("I took a hard left and kept going," that one said). Digital artist Eric Weinschenk had a friend at film school who was dating somebody at a post-production company, and through that route got the introduction for the interview for his first job; after that he worked his way up through the ranks, taught himself software with tutorials, and picked up skills as he went.

All of the visual effects professionals we spoke to agreed that persistence was important, both in moving from job to job and in the willingness to say of your work, *That's not good enough, I can do better.* Other items in the consensus: a digital artist needs a good understanding of art in general — composition, color, lighting — and the ability to translate that knowledge with the digital tools used to create the art. In other words, you need to be someone who knows more than just how the program works. It's like picking up a pencil. Anyone can use it, but it's what you create that matters.

There are more compositors now than there used to be. The market is getting flooded, resulting in more competition for freelance positions on big movies. Also, people are doing effects on digital tape out of their homes now, even considering the daunting hardware requirements and maintenance. But many computer animators lack training in traditional media, and this is a weakness. George Johnsen, head of animation for Threshold Digital, advises young digital artists to learn art history, go to museums, and become skilled at drawing on paper and with paint if they want to break into the digital artist business. Traditional training can only help you in expressing your ideas digitally. The computer is just another kind of paintbrush — if you've got vision and something to say and a context to say it in, you can make something that is thought-provoking and affecting. Or, you can make something empty and technical.

Both animators and visual effects artists also need a strong background in film history, because that becomes the shorthand through which they communicate with film directors. In addition, if you're going to be an animator, in addition to learning computer software you need color theory and art classes: gesture classes, figure classes, and classes in motion. If you can communicate that you can draw, and if a facility likes the image you put in front of them, they will put you in front of the hardware and software they've got. Common animation software packages include Lightwave, Maya, SoftImage, and 3DStudioMax. On the compositing side, leaders are AfterEffects, Digital Fusion, Shake, Combustion, Inferno, and Flame. If you're interested in getting a toe in these waters, you can go to *www.kazaa.com* and download software to practice and teach yourself. While you're surfing the Web, you might want to learn more about Linux, a free operating software program that is quickly spreading in popularity as the basis for animation, compositing, and other post-production programs.

But there's only so much you can do with low-resolution tutorial images, which only teach you an understanding of the program and not so much the application of its tools. If you can work at a company, you'll have the actual images from a project to manipulate. Jobs are not easy to come by, but many artists get their start by interning. "Especially if you're cute," says Weinschenk dryly. "If you're cute, and you want to be an intern, we'll welcome you."

There are also opportunities for writers and writer-directors in digital animation. You should know, though, that the very worst phrase a writer can use in animation is *I don't want the animation to hold me back*, because it means you don't care what the project looks like, and therefore you'll never get another job after this one. As a writer coming to this field, you need to understand animation, the history of what animation is doing, and what the current tools are capable of; also, have some new ideas on how to use them. If you're interested in pursuing this route, watch everything in animation that's been released in the last three years in both movies and TV, and familiarize yourself with a huge amount of classic animation. In-house and in collaboration, animators communicate in shorthand: 1950s versus 1960s Warner Bros., early Disney and late Disney, early and late Bluth. You can use this shorthand as a writer, too, to explain the look you want, because if it's not in your words, it won't be on the screen. And if it's not on the screen, no one will listen to the words.

THE WRAP

> With the line between entertainment and reality becoming increasingly blurred, digital visual effects will change the moviegoing experience in ways we can't imagine yet. Think of movie audiences back in the 1920s, who were amazed by the "visual effects" considered revolutionary for their time. If you asked those 1920s audience members to watch any of today's big special-effects movies, they would probably flee the theater in terror and confusion.

>There is a downside to the perceived ease of digital image manipulation in post-production, since it encourages the natural human tendencies to (A) not bother to do it right the first time and (B) mess with a good thing.

> One of the most frequently accessed and applied visual effects is the process for making digitally acquired images look more like they were shot on film, offering another range of tools and alternatives for moviemakers whose budgets or creative approaches prohibit the use of celluloid.

>Through a combination of hands-on experience and a willingness to work your way up, you can acquire the skills and resume necessary to start a career as a digital artist. However, what many newcomers to the field lack and neglect is a background in, and sensibility for, traditional visual arts and art history, which enhance the creative content, as well as the technical facility of the artist's work.

Mark Greenberg, whose company Xtrackrz produces motion capture with the Jim Henson Creature Shop, is also a filmmaker, and is convinced that the motion-capture technology can be a powerful new storytelling tool, along with the rest of the digital wizardry now maturing. If digital effects are so integral to the future of cinema, why didn't people go see *Final Fantasy*? Greenberg shrugs. "It has to be a good story. Look at *The Simpsons*, which has been hugely popular. The animation quality isn't great, but who cares, because the stories are good. It always comes down to the story."

Final Fantasy's humans, in some ways, were so close to realistic that they were unsettling to watch; technology is still striving to achieve a truly believable digital human, but many wonder why we would need those when we have actors. And people's favorite animated humans — like Homer Simpson, or Belle from *Beauty and the Beast* — are iconic, drawn with simple shapes and simple lines. Everything is shorthand in storytelling, which is a good way to look at the visual effects side of the digital evolution. If it allows us a compelling visual shorthand for the stories we want to share, then more power to all of us.

chapter
eight

>>>*A GENERATION UNREMOVED*

Nowadays, it likely will cost you between $40,000 and $60,000 to transfer a digital feature to film. This can completely obliterate whatever costs you had saved until then. So why do it? If you intend to apply to festivals that only project on film (though those are a dwindling breed), you will need a film print to send them in the event you get into the festival. If you have theatrical release goals, having a high-quality film transfer will affect how your movie is perceived by distribution executives viewing sample works in a screening room. Understandably, many independent filmmakers would only plan and budget for a film transfer if they already had a promise of a distribution deal, or if they were really confident that the movie was going to get a good deal of festival play, for which they would need a very consistent quality on film.

But there's something to be said for investigating all your options, including film transfers, from the moment you decide to shoot. It may force you to make a more careful evaluation of technical and creative choices before you even step on set. And this can only help you in light of the ever-climbing aesthetic bar, as general audiences, industry members and film reviewers now note whether things are shot on video and what the image quality is, since their eyes are being trained to the judge the resolution just like everyone else's are.

In the early days of film, pioneers of cinematic photography had to consult with film laboratories (who were still trying to figure out the chemical processes themselves) on how to shoot and expose properly.[9] The same thing is going on today with digital technology, except that fewer people think to establish a collaborative working relationship with

---

[9] "'Oh... you shot it like that?' Blowing up DV to Film," James Tocher, *MovieMaker Magazine*

a transfer house prior to shooting their movie on DV. Many filmmakers do not get as much image quality as the medium has the potential for, because they aren't properly coached and prepared, and also because they may follow a set of technical specifications from one transfer house and then get their digital movie put on film at a totally different place.

Video-to-film transfer is not a standard lab process. Every company has its own particular way of doing things. If your digitally acquired images are headed for a film output, it's best to pick a transfer facility, consult with it before shooting a camera test, shoot the test DV footage according to their specifications, and then have that DV footage blown up to film so that you can watch the transfer projected on a big screen. All this should be done well in advance of your first day of shooting, and with the collaboration of your cinematographer. If you can find three or four transfer facilities that will offer you a one-minute blow-up test, without sound, for about $200, you can narrow down your choices and, for under $1000, save yourself problems that no amount of money would be able to fix later on.[10]

Some people just go ahead and shoot without that kind of consultation, because they want the democracy of total control over their creation. But people make movies in order for other people to see them, and in order to do that you have to deal with some realities. You want to protect yourself for the idea of blowing up to film. Most of what you learn from a transfer house is to try to strike a balance that will allow you the highest quality image, whether you go for a blowup or not. This means that you want to keep the signal as clean as possible. Don't use in-camera effects when it can be done better in post — even if you want that cheesiness, you can use AfterEffects or Final Cut Pro to add those things without permanently putting them onto your original image. Also, try to get the best video delivery you can in conjunction with transfer-related advice. Shooting at a 16:9 ratio is great if you're only going to be seen in movie theaters, but if you shoot in 4:3 you protect your future for TV broadcasts as well.

---

[10]"The Truth Is In What You See," James Tocher, *RES Magazine*, January/February 2001

Beware of companies giving you very specific lighting advice, because they may be getting ready to do a cheap transfer using a kinescope, which reduces contrast and softens your image. Their lighting advice might be geared to get you to increase the contrast in your images, which will eventually make the kinescope system look better and closer to film resolution. In effect, they're asking *you* to compensate for their problem of not being able to achieve the resolution on their own.

In trying to make video look like film, the biggest issue is resolution, and the next issue is frame rate. PAL and NTSC cameras both capture images in interlaced fields. They don't see motion in the same way that film sees motion. Progressive is the way film sees motion, and you have to use a lot of math, and tricks, to process the images to make one look like the other. Even if it's 24P HD video or 24P mini-DV, these tricks are happening in the transfer process; and because high-definition has so much more resolution in the original image, 24P mini-DV will look more film-like than straight video, but not more so than *The Fast Runner* (shot on 24P HD) after its conversion to film.

Film has much more resolution than video, even high-definition digital video. In lines of resolution, film has nearly 6000 lines of resolution, even as high as 8000 lines for 35-millimeter film. Standard definition video has 700 available lines of resolution, so you're looking at something very low resolution. Then there's the issue of how the format records that resolution, how much video compression happens in the recording process, and what the color sampling rates are. Mini-DV compresses video at a 5-to-1 ratio. Professional formats like Betacam, DVCPRO50, and D9 don't have this compression, and they also give you better color sampling. But even with a different color sampling rate, you still can only get 720 x 486 lines of resolution in NTSC, and 720 x 576 in PAL.

What these numbers mean to you when you go to transfer to film is that you start out with the pixel space limitations of whatever video format you've chosen. Once you've done that, especially with standard-definition NTSC and PAL, you have a problem, because if you try to use your image's pixel to fill up a 35-millimeter negative frame, there won't be enough pixels to go around. So part of the film transfer process is "up-rezzing," or bringing standard definition up to the minimum resolution for film (namely, 2048 x 1536 lines). This means that your transfer company is going to use computers to interpret new information from the existing data to create new lines and new pixels, and expand the image enough to fill the 35-millimeter negative. If your transfer isn't as high a quality as possible, your prosumer mini-DV camera is not going to have an original resolution that will give you anything better than a soft, pixelated image on film.[11]

Because a transfer house wants to start with the cleanest source material possible, the general consensus is that you would *not* want to alter your video footage while acquiring it. Here are general pointers:

> If you have a "true 16:9" CCD camera, shoot with a 16:9 frame. Some cameras pack digital information into a "squeezed 16:9" frame, but this doesn't produce as good an end result, and neither does framing your 4:3 viewfinder for 16:9.

> Unless your camera shoots at 24fps, don't use functions like "frame mode" or "progressive mode" that are meant to make your video footage look more like film. In the short term you'll have a look that may please you on a small monitor, but these image-capture methods cause problems down the road if you transfer to film.

> Avoid other in-camera effects like "sepia," which permanently alter your image and limit your flexibility in post.

> Unless you are shooting in HD, don't use softening filters like ProMists and Soft F/X. You want all the resolution you can get during your initial image acquisition.

---

[11]"Upping the Image Ante: Professional DV Cameras and Transferring to Film," James Tocher, *RES Magazine*, January/February 2002

> Don't use Filmlook, Magic Bullet, or any other kind of software that alters the nature of the video master that you are going to deliver to a transfer house. (If you choose to apply those effects to a video copy to be used for non-transfer purposes, that's a different matter.)

> If your camera allows you a menu option to do this, turn down the "detail enhancement" settings before you start shooting. This is a setting that otherwise can add black lines and white halos to objects, especially high-contrast objects. On a small interlaced screen, these outlines may make the image look sharper, but in a blowup they look bad.

> Don't compress the blacks in your image to the point where you can't retrieve details in dark areas when you get to the final color timing. Again, moderation while capturing the initial images will give you more flexibility later on.

> Have a properly calibrated color reference monitor with you on set at all times while shooting. This way you can get an accurate picture of what the camera is picking up. A wave form monitor will also give you ongoing intensity ratings of the colors in a frame to let you know, whether, for instance, whites are too bright or blacks are too dark for the video to make out detail. Also, if you have to shoot squeezed ("anamorphic") 16:9, you can try to get a monitor that will switch its display back and forth between 16:9 and 4:3 to show you the image both as a squeezed image and as an unsquished, more reassuring one.

> Even better, make this monitor a high-resolution one so that you can minutely check your focus at all times. DV viewfinders and the human eye won't be enough to determine true focus, especially on a close-up, and film blowups are notoriously unforgiving of soft-focused video original. In other words,

what looks a bit soft on a TV monitor will look like it was shot underwater on a big movie screen.

> What you deliver to the transfer house should be a locked-picture, color-corrected video master. They're not going to fix or change colors for you. However, they are in charge of converting your frame rate to 24fps, so don't try to change the frame rate by changing the camera shutter speed while shooting, or by de-interlacing video fields in post.

> Shooting digital NTSC can give you results that are as good as transfers done from digital PAL. NTSC is shot at 30fps, and PAL at 25fps. Because film is a 24fps medium, a video-to-film transfer has traditionally been seen as being easier to originate on PAL. This is not necessarily true. For instance, at Vancouver's Digital Film Group, a proprietary "Smooth Motion" conversion takes NTSC footage and blends the fields, rather than throwing away fields and resolution as some processes do.

> Find out whether the transfer facility uses a recording device that is a "true film resolution" one, meaning that a spot of light on your video image will correspond to the size of a grain of film. The upshot is that, in the end, these devices produce transfers that look more like they originated on film.[12]

So you do all the legwork, you get the fancy monitors, and you follow the advice from the transfer house you've chosen, as far as shooting and posting. What do they *do* for you, now that you've jumped through all their hoops and presented them with your edited, color-corrected movie on tape?

Once you get to the transfer stage, you have a number of different ways to go. At the lowest end of the price and quality spectrum is the kinescope process, which plays back your video on a high-resolution monitor and films it off the monitor. If you take this route, though,

---

[12]Detailed specifications available at *www.digitalfilmgroup.net*

you are limited by the capabilities of the monitor your movie is playing back on. For instance, if by some misfortune the color balance on the playback monitor were skewed all the way to a greenish hue, the film camera would capture it just like that, and then you would have a very expensive, professionally kinescoped film print of a green movie on your hands. More often, the limitation that happens is when a TV monitor can only read so much detail in the black and white areas of your images, the sound is only as good as the speakers playing it, and this imperfect one-time showing of your digital movie is captured for posterity on a very expensive, professionally kinescoped film print. All of this is now considered very old-fashioned.

Electron Beam Recording zaps electrons directly onto film stock, using three different passes for red, green, and blue to reproduce the colors in your images (similar to how a color photocopier or professional printing machine gradually adds colors to an emerging picture). It's a two-step process that records first on black-and-white film, and then makes an optical print (which is not as good as a print developed from a negative) to color film. People don't really do or recommend this anymore, either.

What you want is a digital-to-film transfer facility that will up-rez (increase the lines of resolution of) the video image to 2000 lines before recording out to film. Some houses also add a slight pixel blur to deal with some of problems of interlacing, and some de-interlace the fields from the video capture. Others don't. Cineric, for instance, doesn't do a lot of image processing. They're a dry lab. Their book rate of $295 per minute of footage includes the answer print and soundtrack negative for a feature-length project. At Swiss Effects, the same up-rezzing process gives you a 2K transfer. For a 90-minute digital feature, you'll pay roughly $30,000-$35,000 and wait on a two-week turnaround to get the film negative. After that, you need to allow a week to 10 days to print it, which will entail paying the usual lab costs of a lab near you.

With these film recorders, your footage in its entirety is scanned into a computer, and then re-recorded onto film.   Digital Film Group is another transfer house where they use those fancy 2K film recorders. They take your locked picture, color-corrected video master, and convert your NTSC or PAL material to 24fps using the Smooth Motion process, which DFG developed and owns. After taking your sound off the video master or the DAT or DA88 audio master, they begin making an optical sound negative which will later be married to the picture negative that they produce on their film recorder. In the end you have a "composite print" with a resolution that has been brought up to the 2,000-line resolution of the film viewing experience.   Like a standard answer print, this is a big spool of film that you can actually stick in a theater projector, as opposed to the camera negative, which you can't. After you pay DFG and go home, you will be the proud owner of this color-corrected answer print (it's color-corrected because you started out with a color-corrected video master, but this saves you the time and money of a color timing session in a film lab), your picture negative master, and your sound negative master.[13]

THE WRAP

> A transfer to film can improve the look of your digital video project simply by adding the grain and jitter of celluloid moving through a film projector; part of your pre-production should be to consider whether you want to take this step.

> If you're interested in outputting your digital video project to film, get consultations and comparison blowups from several different transfer houses before you start shooting.

> Understand that one company's recommendations may differ from another's based on the in-house processes they use to transfer your film. Also keep in mind that to go against their recommendations will almost certainly cost you time and money in the transfer process, but will not necessarily prevent your movie from looking the way you ultimately want it to.

[13]"Talking about DV Blow-Ups With Vancouver's Digital Film Group," *www.cyberfilmschool.com*, June 1, 2001

>Tape-to-film transfers are still very expensive, and may or may not be right for your project. For those with strictly limited budgets, it's possible to give the impression of film origination on a video copy of your master by using software like Magic Bullet. Don't alter the master itself, just in case you are hoping someone else will step in and provide you with the finishing funds for a film transfer.

Maybe the numbers sound high and these steps sound complicated, compared to what you originally intended to do. And maybe they don't. As with just about every other aspect of digital moviemaking, the technology available to you only expands your storytelling options. Whether you get your digital material outputted to film or not, doing the research to prepare for the possibility will add to your creative process and allow you to make informed aesthetic decisions. Because you could limit yourself to thinking that you'll never have the need or the desire or the money to transfer your digital work to film — but in a medium where ordinary limitations are cast aside, you might as well cast aside those limiting pre-conceptions as well.

>>>> *Director Ethan Hawke on the set of the digital feature* Chelsea Walls.
Photo: Squire Fox and Stephanie Pequignot. Courtesy of Lions Gate Films.

>>>> *Above: Director Nicole Holofcener on the set of* Lovely and Amazing, *shot in 24P HD. Photo: Alexia Pilat. Courtesy of Lions Gate Films.*

>>>> *Jake Gyllenhaal in* Lovely and Amazing. *Photo: Alexia Pilat. Courtesy of Lions Gate Films.*

>>>> *Above: Anthony LaPaglia and Sigourney Weaver in* The Guys, *shot on film but posted in a digital intermediate format.*
Photo: Robin Holland / ContactFilm.   Courtesy of Open City Films.

>>>> *"Peace Chevy" from* Yank Tanks, *a digital documentary directed by David Schendel.*
Photo: Blue Collar Films.

>>>> *Above: Tomas Milian and Manny Perez in the digital feature* Washington Heights. *Photo: Heights Productions.*

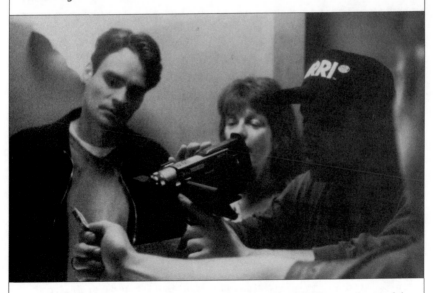

>>>> *Robert Sean Leonard, Ethan Hawke and director Richard Linklater on the set of the digital feature* Tape. *Photo: Clark Walker. Courtesy of Lions Gate Films.*

>>>> Above: The 2003 Sundance Digital Center in Park City, Utah.
Photo: Thom Taylor.

>>>> Hershey's Really Big 3-D Show is the first feature-length original production
showcasing CGI/3-D animation and presented in 3-D High Definition with glasses and
digital projection. Playing daily at Hershey's Chocolate World in Hershey, PA.
Photo: Threshold Digital Research Labs.

>>>> A mobile HD Net control room brings audiences a hockey game in high-definition digital. Photo: HD Net.

>>>> Xtrackrz motion-capture artist Misha Sisti on the stage at the Jim Henson Creature Shop. Photo: Melinda Hsu. Courtesy of Xtrackrz.

>>>> *Vincent D'Onofrio and Uma Thurman in the digital feature* Chelsea Walls. *Photo: Squire Fox and Stephanie Pequignot. Courtesy of Lions Gate Films.*

PART III
MAKING
YOUR
MARKET

chapter
nine

>>>THE MOVERS AND SHAKERS

To paraphrase David Mamet, in Hollywood we allow ourselves to be treated like commodities because we're all hoping that someday we'll be treated like *valuable* commodities.

Here are some sad facts about Hollywood: it's very judgmental, it judges quickly, and it judges on first impressions. When you meet someone on the East Coast, you might ask her where she went to college; when you meet someone in Los Angeles, you glance at her abdomen to see how often she works out. It's *true*. As they say, Hollywood is like high school with money. Furthermore, everyone wants the newest and hottest thing, but no one wants to be the one to take a bad risk on the newest thing that might not pay off.

On the very front lines of how the newest things in town are first seen and shopped around are the agents who represent them. Whether an agent is trying to attach a high-profile client to a DV project to get it funding, or whether the agent is looking at a first-time filmmaker's "calling card" of a finished film shot on DV, agents' perceptions of (and influences on) digital projects are increasingly relevant. As always, the question for filmmakers without agents, managers, or publicists is how to get access to and develop relationships with this often swamped, choosy, and cynical group.

Why get an agent? Agents can help your work get seen, they can lend you legitimacy, and they can make introductions for you; all these things can be critical stopping points in your forward journey as a moviemaker. But plenty of people who have agents aren't working, and plenty of people get their starts in the film industry without the help of agents. So how come successful people always seem to have agents?

First of all, agents, by their nature, gravitate towards successful people. Also, the busier your career is, the more useful it is to have a gate-keeper to field the business of getting you hired and treated well, leaving you to the business of being creative. Or so the common wisdom goes. The truth is that many agents can help springboard your creativity by getting you into collaborations that suit your talents and goals; and the truth is also that every adult artist has final responsibility for his or her own career, creative, financial, and strate-gic decisions. It would be nice if getting an agent meant that you could sit back and let him do all the work, but depending on your busi-ness relationship with an agent, he might only step in where there's an actual contract and money on the table, and everything else up to that point — networking, selling yourself, knowing market realities, and most of all, having the creative goods to back up the talk — is your job.

If they aren't out there doing all that for you, why are agents always so darned busy? A typical business day in the life of an agent starts very early in the morning with cell phone calls in the car to other time zones while on the way to a breakfast meeting. "Meetings," whether over food, alcohol, or bottled water in an office, are the individual chemical reactions that keep the nuclear furnace of the film industry alive. This meeting might be a meet-and-greet where people put a name to a face and establish relationships for anticipated, mutually beneficial collaboration in the future (this is true of every interaction in Hollywood); or it might be a lengthy discussion of notes on a script, feedback on a film, an investigation into both parties' talents and resources; or very infrequently, it might be an actual preparation to sign a concrete business agreement that's about to get the go-ahead.

At the agent's office, meanwhile, the administrative staff and the various agent trainees (a nice label for an underpaid and overworked secretary with enormous ambition) are already at work fielding calls, e-mails, and faxes while they open a deluge of both requested and unsolicited screenplays, screener tapes, and query letters from everyone in the country with a story to tell and access to a phonebook. Most query

letters are just plain ignored, sadly. You can float higher on the submissions pile if you have previous credits or writing and filmmaking
awards to your name — again, perception hinges on having already
been validated by someone else first — but nothing beats a personal
connection to a third party who can then personally recommend you
to an agent. Part of the reason it's so hard to get agents to spend time
on you as a stranger is that so much of their day is consumed by serv-
icing the clients they already have: giving feedback on work in
progress, running down leads on work for hire, returning *their* phone
calls and faxes and e-mails and letters, negotiating on the clients'
behalves, getting payment for work that's been done, and setting up
meetings and introductions so that the whole thing can begin again.

Why on earth would anyone want to be an agent? Believe it or not,
some people thrive on the pace and the constant networking, selling,
wheeling and dealing; also, it can be a way for smart, creative businesspeople to play a crucial role in bringing stories to life for the
audiences of the nation and the world. Also, they get paid on commission. If you've got a client who makes $1 million or $10 million
or $20 million a picture, that can be a nice paycheck for you as well.
To get to that level of influence and income, though, agents have to
be driven, capable, incredibly hardworking and persistent, and lucky
— same as the rest of us.

At any rate, by and large, agents are not going to make extra time to
seek out relative newcomers with a digital story to tell. This is why
your work has to be of a caliber and a spirit to attract them to you.
The good news from a digital standpoint is that making movies on DV
can give you the access and freedom to prove your talents in telling
complete, well-crafted, and visually potent filmic stories. It's easier for
a swamped agent to take a quick break and watch a digital short than
it is for him to sit down and read your feature screenplay when he's
already got a stack of those, long overdue, to be read for people
(clients, collaborators, people who could employ their clients) from
whom he *knows* he has something to gain. And if your digital short is

good enough, the agent will then ask to see your feature script, and he'll have a much better frame of reference for who you are as a storyteller when he sits down to read it.

Now here's a typical day in the life of a manager: same as above, but sometimes with a smaller staff, sometimes working out of a home office, sometimes with fewer clients, usually collecting 15 instead of 10 % on commission, and always without the legal ability to procure employment. Only the last distinction necessarily detracts from their participation in your business life. Many people recommend managers, especially to up-and-coming writers, actors, and directors, since a manager is more likely to have time and a vested interest in nurturing and developing an individual client's work. An agent (especially at the big Hollywood agencies like ICM, William Morris, UTA, CAA, Endeavor and so forth) typically has less time to spend on projects and people who do not have an immediate potential to make a *lot* of money for the agency when it receives its 10% cut. Not to diminish the value of first-time independent projects, but a high-powered agent is usually not going to bother with something that isn't expected to bring in a commission at least in the ballpark of six figures.

Aside from great writing and compelling stories, what agents and managers look for in projects are the same things all other business-minded industry people look for: casting potential, packaging possibilities, target audiences, budget ranges, and existing relationships with production companies and studios.

Managers are more likely than agents to develop a project from its early stages. "Don't smell it; sell it," as agents say; the pressure on them is all about commission, prestige, and volume. So a manager can be a good way to go, especially if your work is in progress and you don't have a long list of credits on your resume. And, if and when you get to the point of needing someone who can legally negotiate a deal on your behalf, you always can find an entertainment attorney or an agent then, and at that point, you'll have money on the table to entice them. It would be nice to think that agents are really only drawn to the passion and vision and intrinsic worth of a story, but the truth is that, like most successful businesspeople, they have bosses, reputations, co-workers, and Lexus payments to answer to.

With all this in mind, why would an agent or manager be interested in a digital filmmaker? For the same reason anyone else in Hollywood is: self-preservation and personal advancement. Non-top-ranked agents and managers face the same hurdles that people in other fields do: how to get noticed, how to make money, how to build a track record so that they'll have more clout in their next turn up at bat. Agents also may be part of an agency that represents other clients (such as actors on your wish list for the starring role in your digital movie) who would work well in a package for an independent film — a package that also would net the agency multiple commissions, prestige, and a measure of creative input. A digital feature or short also can be an effective calling card to get yourself representation. Agents and managers respond to story, craft and voice, so if you do a kick-ass DV feature in those regards, you'll present yourself more favorably than someone who came in with a clunky, unfinished 35-millimeter epic.

Bridging the gap between representation and production is the role of the producer's representative, a focused breed who takes an active part in the creative and business stakes of digital movies from inception to distribution. The affordability of digital image acquisition will make you and your project more appealing to this group, and if you can get one of these people on board, others will respond to the added perception of legitimacy and momentum for your movie.

Whomever you're looking to for representation and practical management, be choosy in deciding to whom you marry your artistic and business interests. It's important to interview prospective agents and find one who believes in *all* your work and talents and goals, not just in the one-shot salability of a particular project. In the meantime, with or without representation, you can help yourself by finding a mentor in the industry to assist you with networking or creative development. Look for people who would naturally take an interest in you and your work, whether because you went to the same school, have a passion for the same subject, or had a nice chat at a mutual friend's barbeque. Also, don't forget that you, yourself, are part of the package you present. If you know in your heart that you are painfully shy and don't know what colors go together in clothing, don't be too proud to go to an acting workshop or an image consultant to polish the way you come across to people. It's a terribly Hollywood suggestion to make, but the fact is that this town judges by style, as well as substance. As for substance, enter competitions and festivals to win awards and thereby make yourself more appealing to potential representation. And most of all, work on your craft, and foster your own growth as a digital moviemaker and storyteller. Use the medium to generate movies that are unique and compelling, and not just *complete*.

When you do walk into meetings with agents, or with anyone else for that matter, make sure they know that you've got your own goals and plan mapped out, that you're going to succeed with or without them, that it's up to them to decide whether they want to jump on this train or not, and that it's up to you to decide whether you want to work with them. All, of course, while being very friendly and non-arrogant and open-minded. And also while being respectful, energetic, entertaining, articulate, and likeable. Keep in mind that an agent must vouch for your personality as well as for your work when introducing you to others. Besides we can't overstate the importance of being on good terms with everyone, always, no matter what.

Finally, in being practical and pursuing the connections that can help you on your way, don't lose sight of the stories that you're telling. Whatever technology you use, people are drawn to what happens next. Technology comes and goes, and tastes change, but the desire to hear a story remains the same. The audience's interest in getting involved in another place, with other characters, remains constant. So it's fine to have a camera, but holding it up and shooting it has to be subservient to telling the story. The movies that work best are always the ones that tell the best stories.

THE POWER OF OTHER PEOPLE'S POSITIVE THINKING

Have you heard the one about the writer who gave a new script to a studio executive, and called the guy a few days later to ask what the exec thought of it? "I don't know yet," he replied. "I'm the only one who's read it so far."

This points to a common theme in the activities of agents, managers, and publicists, as well: their careers are built on trusting — and equally importantly, influencing — the opinions of others. In looking for an agent or manager, to some extent it benefits you to market and publicize yourself the same way you would any other product: create buzz, heat, and the perception that if the other parties don't step up, *they're* the ones who will miss out. It's a lot like dating.

You can't buy publicity — you have to have an angle. Have something to sell, and don't go after publicity just because you'd like to see your name in *Variety*. Have a vehicle and a story. Find people you can trust and believe, and they can alert the media to your story. Use the press for business purposes, though, versus chasing publicity for ego gratification.

Never make yourself look unemployable. If you sell a spec script or make a deal with a studio, coordinate publicity and time of announcements to keep on their good side; let them make the big splash that's aimed at getting actors excited. Don't work at cross-purposes or steal their thunder. Other don'ts: if you're going to be vague, if you're not going to return phone calls, and you're going to be weird, you're not going to get good publicity. As an incentive, keep in mind that writers and filmmakers who can generate, or already have generated, publicity almost always get paid higher salaries.

When Patrick Sheane Duncan (who wrote *Mr. Holland's Opus* and *Courage Under Fire,* among numerous other films) was starting out on the publicity circuit, he asked Robert Redford for advice. Redford's response: Tell the same three stories in answer to whatever question they give you. As if it's your favorite joke, with enthusiasm and care-free energy. It works for politicians, so why shouldn't it for artists?

In other words, keep it simple and repetitive. Later Pat Duncan went on a radio interview with a reporter who told him, during the last five seconds of the countdown to broadcast, that he'd hated Duncan's movie. A second later they went live, and the interviewer led off with the question "So, why do you want people to go out and kill other people?" And Duncan automatically reached for one of his three anec-dotes: "Well, I was sitting in the bathtub and I got this idea for a story...." And it worked.

DO YOU NEED A PUBLICIST?

For an absolute beginner, there's nothing a publicist can do in the gen-eral sense because the media likes stars, and they like something they can latch onto. If every third person in America were picking up digi-tal cameras and hiring publicists, the publicists still couldn't do any-thing for them. Consider the fact that if you have three great scripts and you need to get the word out, what you need is not a magazine article about you but a better agent. (Although don't think that the agent is going to get you great work either. Like we keep saying, get your own work, and the agent will come to you.) If you option or sell a script, sometimes it's to an agency's advantage to publicize those things in the trades, because it makes the agency look good.

The other side of the dilemma is that on independent films, all you have is publicity. If you have a film about to come out, that's the time to try to get publicity because there will be a lot of momentum behind it, and a lot of forces coming together. When promoting your movie, tell peo-ple *who* should see the movie, who it's for, and why they're wrong to think this movie isn't for them. It all helps create interest in you as a commodity, whether it's through the story you have to tell, something unique about your process and struggle, or plain old gossip about moviemaking. Anything to grab a reader's attention in target audiences from *L.A. Times* subscribers to *USA Today* browsers at the airport. Press begets press. Work with someone to build your profile, and know why and how you're building it. Since most people don't read the article past the first paragraph, spin and widespread reach are much more important than the substance or style of the coverage, because you never know what audience is looking at the stuff, and how it might result in work, notoriety, and other payoffs for you. If you find writers in trade magazines or other magazines who are covering stories like yours, do your homework and target them for approach. It's best to come recommended by someone else though, such as a publicist or a studio. Very often if there's a personal relationship between a journalist and a publicist, they trust those publicists and studio marketing executives who have good clients and good stories for them.

When interviewing prospective publicists, let them know you're weeding out companies which you don't see a fit with; make them see *you* as the desirable commodity. Find a connection with people who get your story, people who get so excited that they have to go tell someone about it, too. Look at their other clients, the television and press coverage they've gotten clients in the past, and their overall slate (so that you won't be overshadowed by other bigger projects going out at the same time). Also, find out with *whom* you will work at a publicity firm — whether the person you're meeting with at first, or some other person down the hall.

Ask around, too. Make sure that the publicist has a strong relationship with distributors and can get phone calls returned by studios and can work effectively with them. You want someone who pays attention to every detail, because publicists typically cost about $2500 a month. Usually, what they'll start you out with is kind of a game plan of goals and strategy after an initial brainstorming consultation with you, but this won't provide any guarantees. It's less of a contract per se than it is a campaign plan and a strategic document that also serves as a retainer memo. And if, after several months, the first strategy isn't working, they'll meet again to brainstorm again. Beware of people who make blanket guarantees to you, too (such as, *I can absolutely promise you that your film will get into the Toronto Film Festival because of my fabulous contacts there*). And if a professional publicist tells you that he or she can't do anything for you and would just be taking your money, believe it.

Allow at least three months of lead-time for publicists before your movie comes out, if you want them to do an effective job promoting it. On bigger projects, a publicist's first meeting with a studio or distributor can ideally happen even before photography begins; they'll ask if the production entity has your current bio and headshot, can you be interviewed for the Electronic Press Kit during production, can you be a part of production notes and the DVD commentary, and so forth. Once you start getting contracted for writing and directing work, you can make these terms part of your contract. You can also put in your contract a requirement for an Oscar campaign to be conducted on your behalf — don't think that it's just random selection of whose names and faces you see advertised in the trade magazines under "For Your Consideration" for the Academy Award nominations every year.

THE WRAP

> To find an agent, be someone they believe they can make money off of. The best way to meet an agent is to be introduced and recommended by a third, trusted party.

> Managers are much like agents, except they sometimes take a bigger commission. According to labor laws, they can't procure employment.

> Established publicists (which are the kind you would want, since they're the ones with the contacts and reputations that get their phone calls returned by studio executives and

journalists) cost about $2500 per month. If you don't have a movie coming out in the next three to six months, or if your movie is less than a month away from release, there's not a lot a publicist can do for you.

> Publicity stems from the particular hook you offer the audience, and the effectiveness with which you offer it. Know what and why you're marketing to people, and be simple and repetitive in how you promote it.

Do people with agents, managers, producer's reps, and publicists have a better chance of getting their films made? Not necessarily. Most independent features come into being because a small core of dedicated people didn't let anything stand in their way. With digital technology, there's that much less to stop you from going out and truthfully expressing your voice and viewpoints in images that can reach audiences of all kinds — including, and especially, people from whom you don't need any favors.

chapter
ten

>>>*THE BACKERS*

Digital image acquisition has prompted a return to the DIY (or do-it-yourself) movie, where one person does it all, including the physical production and the camerawork. Many DV filmmakers point to this as one of the medium's satisfactions, since it essentially frees them from having to wait for permission from an outside producer before they go shoot their projects. Even with the blurring line between producers, directors, writers, and actors, though, individual producers and production companies remain integral to the advancement of storytelling on digital video. But though companies continue to spearhead projects with new talent and new voices, most digital producers are no longer inclined to make grand claims about the impact of digital itself in the current economic environment and industry marketplace.

Digital continues to bring people into filmmaking because there's a lower cost of entry. But the studios are starving now for cold hard cash, and little films aren't really bringing that in, so it's still a very uphill climb, even with a proven producer on your side. The real cost of getting a film to an audience is marketing, and those expenditures continue to balloon. On the other hand, producers can help steer your movie to smaller venues and more specific audiences — restaurants, cafes, and dinner clubs that now show digital movies as part of the evening's entertainment, and so on. Also, a producer can help give you the credibility and contacts to broker online rentals and sales. Netflix, for instance, will buy films that haven't had a theatrical release, because their DVD-renting subscribers are always looking for new films.

Keep in mind that many producers are simply storytellers who like to be the ones with the say-so, and digital helps them tell the stories they want to see told. There's a difference, too, between a creative producer who might option the rights to a story or script and then develop that material, an executive producer who can help you get financing for your feature or short, and a line producer who is responsible for all the physical logistics of shooting your movie. In digital moviemaking, guess what, you, yourself, can be all three. And the do-it-yourself route can be a powerful way to advance your own vision and career.

By the same token, there are a lot of people running around Los Angeles and New York with business cards and made-up company names saying that they're producers. Be aware that wherever you live and work, you should present yourself as professionally as possible. Be respectful of other people's time and opinions, return phone calls, have a business plan, and do what you say you're going to do. This sounds incredibly basic, but Hollywood is full of self-declared writer-director-producers with their heads in the clouds, cameras in their hands, and no concrete plan for how they see their projects moving forward. Just because you're in the business of telling stories doesn't mean that you don't face the same adult accountability as people in other businesses do.

In Hollywood, as elsewhere, people respond to the perception of momentum. You'll help yourself by coming across as someone who is going to make the project happen no matter what, someone who is already doing things, and someone who is being sought out by other people. Digital will certainly bring you the first two things, since if you're your own producer, you have control over all aspects of production, including final cut. As for the third, it's up to you to use it as a tool to get there.

WHY DO YOU STILL NEED A PRODUCER?
By "producer" here, we don't just mean your best buddy who owes you a favor and is willing to take on the administrative hassles, crew-hiring, and bad-cop negotiation of your DIY production (although, considering the incredible amounts of time and energy involved in

most shoots, you'd be masochistic *not* to ask for help in these line-producing capacities). Producers, for the sake of the discussion below, are the real deal: entities with proven track records, industry experience, and creative staffs to back them up; people who will instantly lend you and your project credibility, as well as an infrastructure of support and connections.

But wait, you say. *I thought the whole point was that digital video means never having to wait for help.* This is true. DV is much more democratic than film is, because there are fewer barriers between you and the final output. When you do a film finish and you go all the way to a release print, there are many, many steps — negative cutting, answer print, sound print — and they're all expensive. In contrast, digital cameras are making feature shoots accessible to more people, so you have tons of new material, but the story content is usually not as finely developed as that in an expensive film, and these hurried, underdeveloped films are flooding the market. Consequently, it takes longer for good films to float to the top, creating a new and different barrier between your vision and the public's awareness of it.

One way to get over this hurdle is to find a production company to shepherd your digital movie to completion. Independent Digital Entertainment, also known as InDigEnt, came into being in 1999 as a joint venture by IFC Productions, John Sloss, and Gary Winick. They started out with $1 million, in-house cameras and editing facilities, and a mission to produce 10 digital features in the spirit of Dogme 95, each with a budget of about $100,000. The low production outlay was possible because the movies' creative teams agreed to a share in the gross profits in return for their reduced fees up front. *Chelsea Walls*, *Tape* and most famously, *Tadpole*, resulted from these collaborations. But despite the much-lauded return on investment for digital features such as *Tadpole* and *Lovely and Amazing*, other digital production companies have not been as successful as those films' producers (InDigEnt and Blow Up Pictures, respectively). The digital divisions of Greene Street Films, Next Wave Films and its Agenda 2000 production arm have all disappeared after initial flurries of excitement.

However, one company of note in New York is Madstone Films, which hires young film directors and produces their first features on digital video. The company was started by former investment banker Chip Seelig and producer Tom Gruenberg. With directors on staff and all production facilities under its ownership, the company intends to make digital features with creative control from script development to final cut, and then distribute these films to its own theaters, which eventually will use digital projection as well. It planned for its first film, *Rhinoceros Eyes*, to hit theaters in late 2003.

The first-time directors' program at Madstone runs for two years from start to finish. If you're chosen for the program, you get a commitment from the company for a two-year salary, a space to work, and the infrastructure and financing to make your feature. They look at short films from students and from domestic and international film festivals. They also do the usual networking with others in the development world, while keeping their sights open for anything that they think is exciting and interesting, as long as they're first-time feature directors. They're working with a stop-motion animator now, for example, so there's not a particular genre they're oriented toward.

Ideally, a director comes in with a few feature scripts or ideas, Madstone develops the project with him or her, and about a year in, they finance the project. Budgets range from $500,000 to $1.5 million, all generated from private investment. Madstone is a fully integrated production, financing, and distribution company, since they own New Yorker Films distribution company, and run a chain of Madstone Theaters, eight across the country. This provides other streams of revenue to fund the heart and soul of creative development and production.

In approaching Madstone or any other production company to get your digital movie made, you want to make sure the project is as good as it can be, and has as much outside help as it can, because the digital marketplace is flooded from every direction: scripts looking for producers, finished features seeking distribution, distributed films in need of audiences. With these tough realities in mind, says Eva Kolodner, vice president for development and production at Madstone Films, "the worst thing you can do is send me a package that's a lot more hype than content." She would rather have a much more understated, very respectful inquiry letter and some good material that's been developed thoroughly.

"People send a cooler with an icepack and a label 'hot materials inside' — that does not impress me. I don't know who told these people that this was a good idea. But if I get a letter that says, 'I've seen all the movies you've been a part of, I really like your work, and this is why I think you might specifically be interested in my project, for these following reasons' — if they've done their homework and really developed their material, that's great." Kolodner currently is working with someone she found through the cold submission pile. This filmmaker had a letter like that, and then Kolodner saw that her work was at a certain level, and the relationship was built from there.

At Visionbox Media in Los Angeles, the creative teams both produce digital features and also service films that they're not producing. They do everything from making them from end-to-end, to helping them get through production difficulties, to producing post-production. In many of these cases, Visionbox is involved from pre-production and camera choice, all the way through delivery of the finished elements. They don't own production facilities, aside from an Avid and a Final Cut system for solving quick problems in-house. Sometimes projects come to Visionbox ready to go into production and just in need of certain services, or in search of financing. Visionbox is not really in the development business, aside from developing certain projects to produce themselves; usually, they come on board the production before budget is locked or prep is started.

Tortilla Soup was a digital feature that originated at Visionbox with producers John Manulis, Lulu Zezza, and Chris Miller. It was the first digital movie that the Samuel Goldwyn Company made, and HD wasn't an option at the time, but they shot on the Panasonic 480 progressive (now obsolete). Visionbox has also produced a film called *Falling Like This*, which was a mini-DV project. Most often, the filmmaker comes to Visionbox and asks for their involvement, as happened with *Teddy Bear's Picnic*, the Harry Shearer movie about a Republican secret society (also shot on 480P); *Charlotte Sometimes*, directed by Eric Byler about a young man obsessed with his beautiful roommate (and shot with the Sony DSR 500); and *Dopamine*, about a computer programmer who falls in love with one of his own creations, which competed at Sundance in 2003 (after being shot on 780P HD).

Visionbox approaches digital video as a combination of a creative choice and an affordable substitute for film. They help filmmakers find the balance between how much money they're comfortable spending (either because of financing that's already in place, or because of a willingness to go out on a limb), how much they think they can recoup, the needs of the script, and the aesthetic needs of the director. With *Tortilla Soup*, in which Visionbox had an ensemble cast of eight characters (and many scenes with all eight) the decision was made that "film quality" came second to actor performance. This gave them five more days on the shooting schedule, and everyone agreed that it was much more important to give the actors time to perform. In the end, the film was released without telling anyone it was made digitally. Samuel Goldwyn would not allow digital to be mentioned before foreign sales were complete, because, unfortunately, the word "digital" deflates the value of foreign sales.

Like many other digital filmmakers, Visionbox was somewhat frustrated to see that higher-profile digital features like *The Anniversary Party* and *Tadpole* didn't heavily concern themselves with imagery or image quality. Both films had bigger audiences than the typical DV release, and have set other producers back a bit in convincing especially foreign buyers that digital can look as good as film. Meanwhile, *Charlotte Sometimes* received strong critical response for its polished look, and on *Tortilla Soup* the quality of the digital image wasn't even an issue.

When should you approach a company like Visionbox? "Come to us when you're not necessarily financed — because every now and then we help — but when your script and what you want to do is very clear," says Lulu Zezza, chief operating officer and managing producer for Visionbox. In other words, when you can't add anything else, then you need a company like Visionbox to take you to the next step.

Also, keep an open mind about your options, since the digital palette is ever-broadening. Know what you want your movie to look like stylistically, but if you get a producer attached, communicate with him so he can help you figure out what format serves your intentions. You might be thinking you absolutely have to shoot 35-millimeter film because you liked the look of *8 Mile*, but if you express that to a production company, they can let you in on some tricks of manipulating the image to achieve that look, and how you might get there by a digital route. Moreover, before you sit down with a producer, be sure of what's most important for you to protect. Do you want to be able to play with the images in post? Do you want as many hours as possible to work with the cast? Do you really need 65 locations?

Last but not least, don't approach a production company before you're ready. "I can't tell you how often a writer sends a script that's not finished," Zezza says. "And then every few weeks you get the next rewrite. No company has time to read that. If it's a pass, it's a pass."

A pioneer in digital production was Blow Up Pictures, which got its launch at the 1999 Sundance Festival. Headed by Jason Kliot and Joana Vicente, it was the first company to declare an intention to make digital features with its own financing and then form distribution partnerships to get the movies theatrical release. In operating independently all the way to post and their directors' final cuts, the company aims to achieve the level of innovation that makes independent films valuable and unique. Prior to forming Blow Up, Kliot and Vicente had been in the middle of making a film with a big studio, which suddenly decided to push back the shoot from the fall to the spring. They were seeing how studios were making decisions based on finance and not creativity, and they were in the midst of the rise of "Indywood," a flood of independent product with stars attached so that companies could make nice Hollywood films for cheap.

Tired of seeing commerce beat out art, Blow Up's founders realized that digital technology could be the shot in the arm that was aesthetically and creatively needed in independent film. Convinced that with a good story that was appropriate for the digital medium, they could do very well, they produced *Chuck and Buck* after everyone in Hollywood rejected the script about a strangely lovable stalker who is still in love with his best buddy from childhood. They fully financed that feature, announced it in January, shot it in April, had it ready for Sundance in the fall, and sold the distribution rights to Artisan the day after Sundance. Following that, they made *Series 7: The Contenders*, about a reality show where the contestants literally have to kill each other or be killed, and sold it to USA Films and world distribution for a high profit. More recently, they took on *Lovely and Amazing*, which everyone else had rejected because no one wanted to finance it in the current climate. Kliot and Vicente read the script, green-lit it right away, and a year later had sold the feature to Lions Gate after the Telluride Film Festival.

Lovely and Amazing (shot on 24P HD) also had the distinction of significantly outperforming the also digital and much more publicized *Full Frontal* at the box office during the summer both were released. *Lovely and Amazing* was a movie that didn't have any big stars, and no big buzz from festivals or marketing, but it had word of mouth and a good story, and those things got people out to see it. There was nothing visually radical about how *Lovely and Amazing* was shot, and perhaps a Hollywood company would have made it as a film for more money and big stars, but Blow Up persisted in its vision and casting choices. Next up was *The Guys*, starring Anthony LaPaglia as a fire captain who lost eight men on September 11th, with Sigourney Weaver as the journalist who helps him write the men's eulogies. This was shot on film, but then digitized so that all post could be completed on a digital intermediate before finally outputting to a film negative and prints. In following this increasingly popular route, Kliot and Vicente were able to get their project a cinematic quality while still saving money and allowing creative freedom during the post; the film was bought by Universal-based Focus, following the Toronto Film Festival.

Blow Up Pictures wants to make films — digital or otherwise — that are the unique vision of one person, films which no one else would have made. They look for projects that are in some way subversive or pushing boundaries, whether aesthetically, socially, or politically. Plus, there is definitely a new aesthetic that has emerged in the films that they've been making. In the early stages their choices had to do with finding projects that matched the digital look, such as more intimate projects, or scripts that would take advantage of a small video camera being manipulated. Fortunately for *Chuck and Buck* and *Series 7*, the convention of a video image fits into the convention of home videos, television news, and documentary footage, all of which are considered more "real" because of the video quality. Therefore, low-resolution cameras have a tendency to make you feel as if you're witnessing something that's actually happening in front of you. Blow Up chose both *Chuck and Buck* and *Series 7* to use a lower-resolution camera to make the end product more video-like.

Jason Kliot reports that his company now builds reshoots into the production and the budget, so that after editing they can continue to ensure that the director's vision is maintained. The cost of doing that on film would be prohibitive, especially for independents, who are, for the first time, being given an eraser to rework stuff. This can make these digital movies better than they would have been on film. For instance, the use of relatively inexpensive digital stock on *Lovely and Amazing* allowed performances to evolve in a way that they wouldn't have had time to do on film. In addition, there's a nervousness in the storytelling style of *Chuck and Buck* that was achieved by shooting 80 hours of footage, shooting the actors until they achieved the performances and edginess that *Chuck and Buck's* director Miguel Arteta was after.

If you're trying to get financing for your movie, or trying to sell a completed project, Kliot recommends either going for a total no-budget production, or going to a known producing entity with a proven track record, or getting into a festival, which can provide a good impetus for getting people to finish your movie. If you approach Blow Up itself, the worst thing you can do as a new filmmaker is try to sell yourself in a Hollywood fashion. "All of our success comes from the fact that we chose movies that were just *good*," Kliot says. "No stars, no famous people. When someone comes to me and says, so-and-so is famous and will direct it, or is a star on TV, or this is just like *My Big Fat Greek Wedding* — all that is the kiss of death."

THE WRAP

> Digital tools allow you to produce your own movies without waiting for anyone's permission, but the potential downsides of that are the temptation to rush into shooting before your script or creative team are ready, and the probable necessity of putting up the money yourself.

> An established producer can be a tremendous benefit to your digital movie. Legitimacy, production resources, financing, and creative collaboration are the main reasons to team up with an experienced individual or company.

> The best way to approach a producer is to find one with a sensibility and intention that suits your material, do your homework about his or her past projects and track record, and — if you can't get an introduction by a respected third party — make a professional, serious, high-quality submission detailing your proposed project and previous work, and explaining why both are a good match for the producer's own goals.

If you have passion for your movie, and if you truly believe in its story and its potential to affect an audience, then that passion will translate in your discussion with any producer. Temper your passion with intelligence, because unbridled passion is a little bit scary. But if you have integrity, as well as passion, you're going to appeal to producers like the ones we've just discussed. Often, what works financially are movies that couldn't have been made anywhere else by anyone else. And that's what makes for a successful career for a producer and a film-maker in the long run, too.

chapter eleven

>>>*THE POWERS THAT BE*

If you ever want to make (temporary) friends at a Hollywood cocktail party, announce that you're in the business of financing films, and that you have millions of dollars from the late-1990s sale of your software company sitting in escrow just looking for the right director, script, and actor to go make a movie. You suddenly will have more admirers than you know what to do with, and every one of them will have just the right, unmade-but-this-story's-gotta-be-told, movie for you. To quote another David Mamet line, "Everybody needs money. That's why they call it *money.*"

Three major forces come into play when you talk about getting the money for your movie and making your money back: independent financiers, studios, and distributors.

FINANCING YOUR DIGITAL MOVIE
In filmmaking, poverty is not a virtue, in and of itself. Having no cash doesn't mean your ideas are better or purer. On the other hand, having to fight for every penny your project has to spend *does* make you more selective about where you allocate your resources. Don't think of your credit cards as magic money, either. For every Robert Townsend who broke into the business by making an independent film on credit cards, there are thousands of writer-directors you've never heard of because their gutsy independent films didn't get seen, didn't get distribution, and didn't make them a dime back. Since maxing out five credit cards, these filmmakers have been working full-time at boring, soul-draining day jobs just to make the minimum payments every month. And then their dogs all died. Okay, so we're a little gloomy about the credit card route, and we don't mean to stop you from telling your story. But try to use someone else's money if you can.

How can you try to get people to finance your movie? If you are approaching anyone other than your Aunt Sally for investment, then name actors, proven credentials, and viable market potential will help them see you as a reasonable investment risk. It also helps to have an amazing script and a powerful story and the passionate desire to see your movie get made. And often all of these factors can be present, and it's still hard to find the money. This is when you have the opportunity to work on the two things that will lead to the most effective return on investment: refining your script, and keeping costs down. The better the script is, the better the movie will be. The less you spend, the less you have to pay back. Sounds like a simple formula, but thousands of mediocre, over-budget, unseen independent features prove that it's much easier said than done. And one of the pitfalls of digital technology, with all its ease and immediacy, is that it allows filmmakers to rush into a do-it-yourself shoot before they, their scripts, or their creative teams are truly ready.

Also, be careful what you wish for. It's appealing to imagine a dot-com escapee playboy with cash burning holes in his pockets meeting you in a buffet line and inking a financing deal with you on a cocktail napkin by the time the two of you have reached the dessert platters. This may seem like an ideal situation. However, go into such a thing, and into any financing arrangement, with your eyes open. There are whole books on the subject of film financing, but to put the following discussion in a context of existing practices, we want to lay out a quick rundown of the current landscape.

Here are some of the reasons why more money may mean more headaches for you as a filmmaker and storyteller:

1. When someone gives you money to make your film, unless it's an outright gift, at some point you're supposed to give the money back.

2. Investors invest money because they'd like to get the same amount or more back. Otherwise they'd call it a charitable donation. Which is another way to go, but to do it legally you need to find a not-for-profit organization willing to sponsor you and your project. Usually that means hoops, paperwork, and an administrative fee taken by the umbrella organization in return for disbursing the money and monitoring how you put it to use.

3. Limited partnerships can be formed out of groups of investors who get part ownership of the product in return for their cash, but you need to hire a lawyer and be seriously accountable (meaning, follow the federal regulations of the Securities and Exchange Commission) for how you approach people and how you deal with the money you collect.

4. If you don't have to give the money back, it's because you've already handed over your pound of flesh instead. Some elements of that pound of flesh might include, but are not limited to:

    > Distribution rights – pre-selling these used to be one of the most popular ways to get up-front financing for an independent feature, but this market has gotten much, much tougher with the times. You should be so lucky that this is what you're trading for cold cash or a paper contract that can be used as collateral in a bank loan.

    > Producer credits – most rich people need more than the vanity appeal of seeing their names on a movie screen to convince them to give you their money, but a producer credit (or a co-producer or associate producer credit) can help sweeten the pot.

> > Creative control – one of the most hotly contested issues in any film, no matter what size. It's why directors like John Sayles have funded films out of their own pockets, in order to have final say on everything. Very often the flip side of financial support is that the person with the checkbook gets power over casting, artistic choices, and final cut. This can be a hefty price to pay for the financial freedom to get your movie shot. On the other hand, it beats not getting the movie shot at all.

> > Back-end participation – whether this comes out of your gross or net, you can court potential financiers with pieces of the eventual pie in rental revenue, distribution sales, sequels, video games, plush toys, and whatever else you can sell or license in order to continue squeezing money out of your creative vision.

5. Nobody trusts anybody. Especially where money is concerned.

6. Completion bonds are required for projects that have a lot of money riding on them. This means that you have to take out a sizable insurance policy to guarantee your investors that you will either finish the film or, in the event that your budget skyrockets and your production slows to a crawl, be compelled to turn control of your movie over to the bank so that the bank can try to get it into some kind of shape where people have a realistic hope of seeing their money back. As you can imagine, having the bank shut down production does not lead to a fertile creative environment for the film from that point onward. For this reason, some directors try to avoid shooting the conclusion of the film until the last possible moment, in an effort to convince the bank that stopping photography would leave the film without an ending and therefore un-salable, which would be an even worse option than letting the director slog onward.

7. For non-guerrilla-filmmaking purposes, a grand variety of other insurance, such as errors and omissions insurance to address lawsuits in the event of your unintentional mistakes that result in legal action against the production, is required to convince investors that they're not opening themselves up to legal liability just by having their money and names associated with your project. If you don't feel like tempting fate, you'll also want a workers' compensation policy, general liability coverage, and insurance on everything you rent, borrow or shoot inside of for the duration of the production.

8. People can change their minds about loaning you money.

   > Investors pull out all the time. If they're smart, they won't sign or hand over money until the last second, and they'll give themselves a way out if they suddenly decide that they'd rather take that trip to Aruba instead. Usually, you won't have any recourse to hold them to their original cheery promises, and you'll be left swinging in the wind or scrambling to make up the loss.

   > Even if they're not given to fickle whims, people with financial leverage over you will design agreements so that you have to satisfy their various requirements, and if you don't live up to your end of the deal, they can withdraw their money, support, and name from your project.

9. You, on the other hand, can't change your mind about giving people the money you promised them.

   > If you borrow money from a bank (not to mention from a credit card), you'll repay it with interest. Declaring bankruptcy is not a good fall-back plan, especially if you want to do anything like find a new apartment, house, car, or significant other in the meantime.

> Pay-or-play deals with actors require you to give them every penny of the agreed-upon amount whether you end up shooting your movie or not. Sometimes this is the only way to ensure that you'll get the actor you want, but it also opens you up to the possibility of getting nothing for money that you definitely will be spending.

10. Nonrefundable deposits are exactly that — on stage rentals, costumes, props, equipment, you name it. A soundstage doesn't care if you had a fight with your writer or if you got evicted from your apartment. Once you sign over a security deposit to any normal business, you give them permission to keep your money.

All that said, there are people out there right now putting money into movies with the expectation of seeing their money back, if not back with interest. So what gives those people confidence that they're not throwing their money into the sea?

Some people really do believe in the power of a particular story, especially if it's one that is intensely personal to them. Other times, the project is sometimes seen as an almost guaranteed return on investment due to certain salable elements: sex, name stars, violence, genres (like horror) that translate across cultures and languages. As you read this, somewhere in Eastern Europe there are fairly big-name movie actors filming "B" grade shoot-em-ups with studios, locations, and crews that cost a fraction of their equivalents in the United States, and those movies will have made their money back on video sales even before they've wrapped shooting. And sometimes, people are in the business of believing in their creative team, either because the team has a proven track record or because it's to the financier's benefit to publicly foster new talent. Usually in Hollywood, it's some combination of all of the above.

There's a bumper sticker that says *I know money can't buy happiness, but I want to find out for myself.* If you're still on the lookout for the financing for your digital feature, the bright side of having to search for the money is that it should make you spend more time developing your script and planning your pre-production, which in turn will give you a better product in the end, which in turn will give you a better shot at making your money back. And even if you can secure financing, don't feel like you need to push the budget to its limits. The less money you spend up-front, the quicker your investors make their money back, the quicker the movie turns a profit, and the quicker somebody steps up to support your next project. Either way, one of the greatest things about digital is that you don't have to wait for anyone's permission to go tell your story.

STUDIOS

It's *so* easy to bad-mouth the studios. Everybody does it. Independent filmmakers and their proponents are often heard saying that studios are close-minded, over-spending, nepotistic, change-resistant, lowest-common-denominator-targeting, greedy, archaic, and unfair stoppers of creative currents (even though the studios continue to be integral to some of the most fundamental achievements and infrastructure of cinema today). Kind of like how everybody complains about paying taxes, but nobody objects to having roads. Maybe the government overpaid on the asphalt, or took too long to fix those potholes. But at least they're equipped to get the job done. Ego, politics, hubris, greed, fear, and ignorance all drive the film industry. But it's also tough to think of a for-profit industry that is *not* significantly affected by these fallibilities.

In the studio system, people do recommend their friends for opportunities, they do try to rack up and repay favors, and there is an extreme wariness of looking stupid or mismanaging money. This is basic human behavior. So let's not get on our high horses about the faults of those at the studios. It's just that their survival instincts and group dynamics are reinforced by massive corporate structures, are playing out on a very, very large scale with extraordinary financial stakes, and have taken on a life of their own, with a resulting impact on a great number of movies that get made and seen.

If there are any entities known for their focus on the bottom line, it's the Hollywood studios. They are interested in DV for more than that, but cost savings have certainly given them a reason to explore the format sooner rather than later. Studios aren't just concerned with features, either. Many television shows shot at studios are switching over to high-definition digital acquisition — usually 24P — although this is not necessarily netting them significant cost savings; the current estimate is that switching over a $1 million episode from film to digital production saves the studio $3000. Post processes are still expensive, and many of the fixed costs like actors' salaries and producer overhead remain the same. The only thing that's undeniably cheaper is digital stock. However, this move towards digital origination will leave studios in a better position as TV broadcasting standards change over to digital rather than analog broadcasts.

Two of the biggest considerations for studios, in choosing how to originate and store their content, are longevity and standards. Studios are interested in exploring what will complement the production and exhibition process without compromising it. And they're also thinking about what to put in the vault for posterity. In this respect, the cautious pace of individual studios and the Digital Cinema Initiatives consortium (set up to determine and establish digital projection standards) is a good thing. First of all, it'll be worth the wait for digital capture and projection to get to the point where it's showing 4000 lines of resolution, instead of caving in to pressure to settle for the current technology's capability (in other words, a 2000-line standard), which will soon be outmatched by HDTV sets available to audience members in their own homes.

Furthermore, the film industry has been burned before in the push to get the latest and greatest technology out onto the consumer market. Years ago, when DVD technology was coming to maturity, a headlong rush to start marketing DVD titles and players resulted in the hardware not truly achieving the standards the studios were supposed to have established. Software patches and ongoing quality assurance expenditures have to compensate for these hardware glitches, with the end result that the net profit from a DVD rental is proportionately much less than the net profit offered by a VHS rental. Hindsight now tells us that if the studios had platformed DVD and nursed it along while figuring out the kinks, both the industry and the audiences would have been better served.

Finally, it's important to take the hype surrounding studio efforts with a grain of salt. Studios, like any other players dealing with large economic forces and stakes, put their own spins on marketing campaigns. For instance, the crowd that was going to see the *Star Wars* re-release was generally content to hear about the digital aspect of the restoration without investigating the specifics of what portion of the restoration was actually done with analog methods. Also, studios are dealing with big companies that also have enormous amounts of money and public perception at stake. Often, what's really going on behind the scenes is one thing, and how technology holders and the media portray it for their own purposes is another. In short, when you hear sweeping statements on digital technology from a representative of a company, keep in mind what that company is also promoting — whether it's cameras, software, feature films, or the perceived value of stock shares.

But before we descend utterly into anti-capitalist cynicism, we'll end on a hopeful note. Studios and technology holders also have it in their power to provide us with an untapped wealth of older films that can be digitally restored and brought back to audiences. A recent restoration of *Singing in the Rain* started out with Technicolor 3-strip (RGB) negatives. Digital scans of the negatives were each recorded at 2K resolution, and then software re-registered the images and exactly matched them to each other for a full-color print. As a result, this copy of *Singing in the Rain*, shot in 1952, can be projected at a higher resolution than *Episode II: Attack of the Clones*.

What's really exciting about these restorations is the expectation that it will one day be very inexpensive to digitally broadcast old films like *Lawrence of Arabia* or *Roman Holiday* to theaters, especially smaller theaters in little towns where ordinarily you can't get this kind of material, and then switch them into the theater's programming on "off nights" such as Monday and Tuesday, before digitally switching back to the latest mainstream release. Thanks to the studios' current investments in digital technology and their previous investments in film libraries with thousands of titles, there's a whole new life ahead for classic films and the audiences who wouldn't otherwise have had a chance.to see them in the theaters.

DISTRIBUTORS

After Artisan's remarkable profits from *The Blair Witch Project*, the initial apparent goldmine of DV and other mixed media films has given way to a more complex reality of the limited space available to even mainstream studio releases, as well as the growing glut of both digital and celluloid films reaching festivals and film markets every year. Say the market can only handle four or five hundred movies a year. Independents are making four or five *thousand* movies a year. Which means that most movies can't find a real audience. They won't pay for themselves on any basis. And imagine what it's like to be a distributor, facing this swamp of four thousand new movies every year. How do you get your movie to rise to the top of that pile, when thousands of movies are vying for attention from the same people?

Typically, what the market does is look for built-in film placement systems. First of all, how many festival awards you've won. Secondly, whether big-name actors are in your movie. And third, whether you have a producer's rep or an agent adding caché to your project. A high-powered producer's rep like Jonathan Dana or John Sloss, or a well-connected agent like Robert Newman or John Ptak, has a reputation for not getting involved with a movie unless it's of a demonstrable quality and potential.

As far as whether digital origination adds to the value of the movie, or is downplayed to increase the perception of legitimacy, a distributor just wants to sit down, look at the movie, and if it looks good and has all the other promising pieces in place, they'll buy it. If you can make it look good in digital, they don't care. Audiences don't respond to digital as a marketing hook per se, either. The audiences respond to what they see, and what they really want is a great story. However, one of the challenges with digital origination is that it often complicates delivery of your movie (such as music-and-effects soundtracks, optical elements), particularly overseas, since many foreign distributors have very difficult delivery demands in terms of specific items and quality standards.

One movie that did well in theaters without any mention of being shot on digital was *Lovely and Amazing*, a drama about a mother and her body-image-obsessed daughters. Producer Anthony Bregman put the project together without the intention of shooting digital; director Nicole Holofcener always wanted to have it look like film, since her style is based on story, characters, and acting. But having gone out to backers with the intent of shooting on 35-millimeter film and not being able to set it up financially, Bregman then found fans for the script in Jason Kliot and Joana Vicente at Blow Up Pictures. They said they would fund the film, but for a smaller budget and a digital shoot. Eventually, *Lovely and Amazing's* 24P HD film transfer was virtually indistinguishable from features that originated on 35-millimeter film, and the modest production budget made its money back in a successful theatrical release. Bregman and his team not only intentionally downplayed the digital aspect in terms of promoting the film, but with the shooting and the style that Holofcener wanted.

THE WRAP

> People who have money usually didn't get it or hang onto it by accident. Smart investors are tight with a dollar, and you have to present them with good reasons to part with their money, even temporarily.

> Along with incentives to put up the money for movies, all financing entities will want something even better in return, whether it's creative control, back-end profits, or a hoped-for return on investment that allows greed to overcome caution. Usually the last.

> If you're in a position where you need to use credit cards to get your movie made, think long and hard about how you plan to pay back the credit card companies if bags of money don't start falling from the sky.

> Advances in digital image acquisition have not truly changed the economic realities of working in large corporations such as studios or distribution companies. If anything, the new influx of digital product has made acquisitions executives even more reliant on traditional winnowing — looking first at festival awards, producer's reps and name actors — to sort through the new movies arriving every day. Which makes it even more difficult for new movies and new names to get noticed and shown in theaters.

Anticipated return on investment is the key consideration for any individual or company who funds or distributes films. Since DV projects usually require a lower initial investment, the odds are that much better for backers who hope to realize a profit on the money they provide up front. Investor opportunity and artistic ideals can complement each other, as they did in the financing of Dogme's *Dancer In The Dark*, which brought in support from over two dozen European film organizations, as well as the U.S.-based Good Machine.

Meanwhile, long-term investments of a different type also make it worthwhile for companies like Madstone Films to foster the growth of individual directors who, if not for more affordable DV productions, might have had to wait much longer for a chance to tell their stories. While mentorship and creative relationships are desirable and commendable, though, for many financiers — particularly non-U.S. ones seeking co-production roles — what determines a project's viability is always going to be the risk versus reward in dollars and cents. Digital video, properly used and presented, can reduce those risks and promise the rewards.

chapter
 twelve

>>>*THE LOW-DOWN ON DOWNLOADS*

Let's face it — part of the appeal of digital, especially on the low-budget end, is that it brings filmic storytelling within reach of a lot of people who wouldn't have had the resources otherwise. The idea of seeing your images, your words, and your story on a giant screen, shimmering in front of an audience of all the people who scorned you in
high school and all the relatives who couldn't figure out what you
were doing for a living, is seductive. And that kind of inspiration can
be valid and useful. But the cold truth is that many of these images
end up not projected on a theater screen, but confined to a videotape
box, or hidden on a computer hard drive. Better those places than just
your mind's eye, to be sure. However, in an effort to avoid the pitfalls
that make it more difficult to find viewers, it's never too early to plan
for the distribution of your self-made digital movie.

Even if Sundance and Miramax don't turn you into the latest
Hollywood ending, don't underestimate the value of writing a tight,
compelling script. Audience word-of-mouth is very often the best
publicity, and most sleeper hits have enthusiastic viewers to thank for
propelling them into the spotlight. In other words, don't assume that
because you're passionate about the story, other people will automatically become so. They have to be brought there by you, and the first
tool you have is your script.

Also, be aware of the long road leading to self-distribution. If it were
really that easy, we'd see a lot more self-distributed films making their
way to audiences and profitability. The latter usually remains elusive
for people making their own films, and sometimes the former does as
well. What many people don't realize when they get into this is that
you're married to the movie you create. It does take a big toll on your

life, and sometimes you can get the frustrating feeling that since nobody has seen your movie, it's almost as if you never shot it at all.

DO-IT-YOURSELF DISTRIBUTION

Once in a great while, a *Blair Witch Project* comes along, with unknown filmmakers and actors finding exactly the right time and audience for their completely independent project, repaying their investors, winning fame, and ensuring their next jobs. These success stories give all creative people hope. But a more typical journey is taken by first-time filmmakers who shoot on digital video, spend a year or two sending their projects out to film and video festivals, as well as domestic and international "B" grade video distributors, and then receive no response from anyone. Still, it's possible to give copies of these movies to mom-and-pop video stores and local retailers, although Blockbuster Video won't accept that kind of walk-in.

Also, some people find an important freedom and benefit in distributing their own movies. Steven Raack's digital feature *Life Is An Attitude* profiles Ron Heagy Jr., a quadriplegic motivational speaker who founded a not-for-profit camp that serves disabled children and their families. Through an Internet site, Heagy's company has sold thousands of copies of the documentary, which continues to reach a growing audience. Raack made the 80-minute feature for $61,000, about $15,000 of which was spent on the transfer to a 16-millimeter print.

Aside from people with their own Web sites, there are countless others who are selling their own features and shorts through online stores from Amazon to E-Bay. So what's the missing magic ingredient that stops new filmmakers from turning their project into the next *Blair Witch* or *My Big Fat Greek Wedding*? It's not money; look at the millions poured into the promotional campaigns for *The Mothman Prophecies*, *E.T.: The Extraterrestrial's* 20th anniversary re-release, *Treasure Planet* or any other big Hollywood effort that didn't make its money back at the box office. It's not star power; look at *Collateral Damage*, which proved that even Arnold Schwarzenegger can't force people to buy tickets. This is not to knock any of the above movies, because the missing element is the perception that it is necessary to make time to see a certain movie. And that's increasingly difficult these days, with the lack of leisure time and multitude of other and cheaper distractions pulling at potential audience members. Sure, people still went to see movies during the Great Depression; but those people didn't have e-mail, voicemail, Playstation, multiplex parking garages, or five hundred television channels to distract and deter them, either.

Leaving aside for a moment the hectic complexity of the modern world, let's get back to this idea of creating urgency in the potential audience member's mind. One way to do it is by blanketing the media with advertisements and making it so that the average citizen sees a poster or a commercial for the film half a dozen times during the course of a day. For most people, this is far too expensive to undertake. The opposite end of the spectrum is the grassroots approach, for instance through a please-watch-my-movie e-mail campaign, which will have about the level of effectiveness of any other type of electronic spam. In between these two extremes is culling an audience slowly on a small scale, and expanding outward to meet the demand. The momentum of this spread can be accelerated by positive publicity from a festival, awards the project has won, or any other easily communicated hook to get people's interest — for instance, "This is a film by and about Native Americans," which helped audience members make a quick decision about whether or not they were interested in making the time to see *Smoke Signals*. If your movie is playing in a theater, enough audience members have to be deciding in your favor for the exhibitor to want to keep your movie on the screen instead of replacing it with one of the hordes of competitors lined up for screen space.

If you're not shooting on digital video purely to experiment for and entertain yourself, one way to help an audience find your project is to be very clear, from the beginning, who is going to want to see the completed movie. It's nice if your themes and stories are so universal that every human on the planet is going to have a vested interest in sitting down and watching, but chances are your story is going to have more appeal for some people than others. At the very least, know who this subset of the population is, and tailor your communications to them, while saving time and energy by not casting an unrealistically wide net. And if you haven't locked your shooting script yet, strongly consider who your eventual audience is going to be, especially if this is a first feature. It's always going to be important to stay true to your vision and the story you want to tell. But if you want more than a close circle of friends to line up and buy tickets or DVD copies to see your work, it's very valuable to be realistic about how you approach a project as well.

This includes addressing a number of factors that are under your control before, during, and after shooting. You'll need to apply common sense and legwork before approaching the outside world with your product. Don't let your digital movie suffer the unfortunate fate of *Superstar*, the unauthorized biography of Karen Carpenter acted out entirely with Barbie dolls and voice over. This affecting and extremely well-directed film will never be seen except on forbidden underground copies, since both Mattel (makers of Barbie) and the Carpenter estate took swift and effective legal action to prevent the film from ever being shown in public.

Copyright and right-to-privacy considerations apply to your movie, whether it plays in a theater, on the Internet or on the TV at your neighbor's house; and if you're trying to make money on your movie, you can run into serious financial and legal problems when you try to use music, musical performances, other film footage, recognizable products or brand names, and a host of other things you probably didn't even think weren't available for free use. For instance, the rights to the song "Happy Birthday" belong to Warner Bros. (which is sometimes why it's replaced with "For He's a Jolly Good Fellow," which is in the public domain), and Mattel not only charges licensing fees if a Barbie doll appears in a film, but the company has a set of guidelines governing how Barbie can be seen — guidelines such as, *boys don't play with Barbie* — consistent with the public image of the product. So, if you don't want to pay extra money or go through legal channels, don't open your film with a boy singing "Happy Birthday" to his Barbie collection.

The point is that self-distribution is not just about getting the word out to people and having a good product to show them if they come to you. It's also about having a product that isn't going to get you, or a potential distributor, into trouble with the law or severely in debt to the owners of copyrighted and trademarked items that you have appropriated for use in your for-profit endeavor ("Fair Use" for educational purposes and certain other limited venues is a different matter). You can make your own life easier by using music in the public domain, not photographing any brand labels or easily recognizable products, not using footage clips or still photos that weren't created by you, and getting every single person who works with you on the project to sign a deal memo outlining contributions and compensation. If your actors and crewmembers belong to guilds, follow the union rules that apply to them and to your shoot. All of this advance work, while requiring vigilant attention to detail on set, will be well worth the savings in clearance hassles and future lawsuits.

It also will make you look more professional to whoever sees your movie, particularly to those who might be interested in paying you money to distribute it themselves. Imagine that you're showing your feature to some big cheese at a distribution company, and she says, "Wow, how'd you get the rights to that Barry Manilow song that your hero lip-synchs to during the climactic car chase?" and you have to admit, "Actually, we didn't get the rights, we just used the song because we never thought we'd get this far." First of all, you just raised the price of your film by about twenty thousand dollars, assuming you are allowed to keep the pivotal scene in at all. Even worse, you've made yourself look unprepared and amateurish to a businessperson who you are asking to stake a considerable sum of money, as well as a personal reputation, on your project. And if you didn't think to clear something as glaring as a Barry Manilow song, what else might you have missed? Don't think that without brand names and the pop songs your movie won't be as good. Either those copyrighted items really are integral to the story and deserve the proper clearance process and fees; or your story isn't strong enough to come through in the midst of generic toys and original music. If the latter is true, you should be revising the script instead of worrying about art direction and music choices.

GETTING SOMEONE ELSE TO DISTRIBUTE YOUR MOVIE FOR YOU

But let's assume you've done everything to make your story as compelling as possible and all your contracts and rights clearances are in place. What now? In taking your digital movie out to the viewing public, should you even tell people that it was shot digitally, if it's not immediately evident on screen or critical to the story? To be perfectly honest, "digital" is not the best, or first, selling point to use. Yes, people are saying that it's becoming an aesthetic non-issue these days and that we're going back to a content-based evaluation of what appeals to distributors and audiences, but the cold truth is that to most people the word "digital" is still equated with "low-budget," and especially outside the United States, it can cause a quick loss of interest from potential distributors. This is all assuming that you are like most filmmakers and would truly prefer for someone else to provide the money, infrastructure, and negotiating power in getting your film in front of audiences.

How do you find these distributors, aside from the phone book? There are certain places their representatives congregate, notably at film festivals and annual film markets such as the American Film Market, MIFED, and the IFP Market. There are also producer's representatives who can try to broker these meetings on your behalf. If you already have established producers working with you, it helps to be introduced or be accompanied by them in order to prove to the other party that you're not just a new kid from nowhere. Again, it's like high school, but it's also a way to establish your credibility to a guarded stranger whom you're asking for money and commitment.

In approaching distributors, you can send them tapes or DVDs of trailers or finished projects, and you can also invite distributors, agents, and other potential sources of assistance to a screening that you arrange yourself. The problem is that once you rent a movie theater for $3000 or so, the hard part is getting your audience to come sit down and watch it with you. In your friendly hometown, you may get a cheering crowd with standing room only, but there might not be anyone local who could take your project to the next level. On the other hand, in the heart of Los Angeles, where you can hardly get out of your car without bumping into someone who might be able to give your filmmaking career a boost (or at least people who say that they can), you can send out hundreds and hundreds of invitations, and still get only a few people to actually make it all the way to the screening room. Even if it's a nice screening room in an easily accessible part of town. Even if you provide free parking, and hors d'oeuvres. It's a tough town. It's the old dilemma: how do you get word of mouth on something that people won't see without hearing about it through word of mouth?

The Internet is another way to spread the word, although the phenomenon of *Blair Witch* advance publicity should be seen as just that: a happy aberration that can encourage the rest of us without deluding us into thinking it happens more than once in a blue moon. But if you're trying to send footage directly to viewers, even through a higher-profile site like Ifilm or Atomfilms, a major problem with the Internet is that most people's computers still lack the speed to download or stream your short film without sometimes significant delays. Even if you find viewers with the patience to focus on a little square of their computer monitor and not move, the quality of the images they see, not to mention the sound, is likely to be much less than what you were actually able to create, and therefore won't do your story or your talents justice.

If you do choose to send out your work this way, you'll have to encode it using MediaCleaner or a similar program. Unfortunately, your digital movie will suffer more compression in the process. But you can encode it into a downloadable or streaming format, creating a compressed video file that can be sent out over the Web via a server to a Web site. Audiences can then watch your movie on a viewer such as QuickTime, RealOne Player (formerly known as Real Player) or Windows Media, either on a purely streamed format, a streamed display that is broadcast as enough of the download arrives incrementally, or from a file that they've downloaded onto their own computers. Once your file is downloaded, the audience member has it, period, so if you're concerned about piracy the best way to go is a pure stream (though not everyone will have the hardware to get a satisfying viewing experience from this). You can also offer video clips through a site like *www.kazaa.com*, which is a hub site for peer-to-peer sharing. Unlike Napster, Kazaa is not providing the content, they're just providing the portal for you to get through, and they're not making money from it.

Does self-promoted word-of-mouth ever work? Absolutely. The cartoon series South Park got its start as an underground animation short (a gift "holiday card" for a Fox exec who liked Matt Stone and Trey Parker's talents) about a battle between Jesus and Santa Claus, showcasing the South Park gang and an animation style that have become so widely known. This extremely irreverent and cheerfully subversive product grabbed the attention of executives and assistants all over Hollywood and made them laugh out loud. As a videotape copy, it was also something that could be handed from one person to another, and something that could be quickly, easily, and cheaply bootlegged in the vast array of dubbing stations throughout Los Angeles. The day is not far off when DVD copies will be just as universally easy to burn in your office or home; and until then, there's a lot to be said for giving people a videotape that doesn't require them to make any extra or different kinds of efforts before they're able to plop down on a couch and look at it.

Also, make sure people know what they're getting. A great film such as *Iron Giant* did badly at the box office partly because people were shown a trailer that made them go to the movie thinking it was going to involve a giant outer-space robot shooting at things and showing his bag of tricks, and instead it turned out to be a fairly sentimental drama about tolerance and the Cold War. The advance materials for *The Blair Witch Project*, the classic example, were able to generate an Internet following through a creepy site, but they were also telling you over and over that you were going to see amateurish looking footage of freaky stuff happening to normal kids, and that's exactly what you got. *Bowling for Columbine* was a sleeper hit fueled by audience members telling other like-minded audience members that they had to go out and see this well-made and highly entertaining commentary on violence, the media, and fear in America, while audiences dismissed *Full Frontal* because of the gap between their expectations of a star-studded cast led by Julia Roberts, the latest Hollywood films they'd seen from its director Steven Soderbergh (those being *Erin Brockovich*, *Traffic* and *Ocean's Eleven*) and what they got: namely, an experimental, introspective, and unglamorous-looking exploration of a voyeuristic tale.

Even with all the above pieces in place, sometimes the deciding factor in distribution is not how good the film is, but what the market will accept that year. Certain films just hit at the exact right moment in time, like *sex, lies, and videotape* or *The Blair Witch Project*. The downside of that for you as a filmmaker is that these newest-thing-in-town trends are not predictable. The upside is that you yourself could become the newest thing in town. And one way to be discovered for that purpose is to get your work shown and seen at festivals.

FESTIVALS

Applying to festivals is a time-consuming and expensive process. In your original production budget, be sure to allow for entry fees, video dubs of your movie, copies of marketing materials, and shipping costs. Also budget travel, lodging, and daily expenses for when you do get into a festival and then need to attend it. But it's well worth it to set this money aside, because festivals are still one of the very best ways for new filmmakers to get seen, noticed, and hired for their existing or future work.

Festivals, especially high-profile ones like Cannes, Sundance, Toronto, and Berlin, are deluged with entries from all over the world, and their selection committees are under a host of pressures to find projects that will make them look good, as well as continue to further the festival's goals. When submitting to highly competitive festivals, it helps to have an advocate on the programming staff. It would be unfair to say that nepotism is the governing force or the only way that these festivals make their selections, but it would also be naive to say that all films start out equal in the eyes of all judges. A reviewer on a festival committee will become more interested in your movie if you have name stars, established producers, a distribution deal, a track record as a director or writer, a personal connection to the festival's decision makers, a marketing hook, other awards or credentials, and a particular fit for that festival's image, roughly in that order. It's like dating: the more you appear to be sought after by others, the more desirable you seem to the next person you meet.

Aside from having a connection within the festival or movie stars to get your digital feature noticed, another good strategy is to start out small, with up-and-coming festivals that truly suit your material's niche or your own geographic, ethnic, and artistic background, and then use credits, reviews, and awards from those smaller festivals to beef up your resume as you start applying for larger and more prestigious festivals. (Incidentally, the same goes for funding grants offered by a variety of not-for-profit but highly respected organizations.) If you see festivals as being your primary means of exposure after your movie is finished, take a day or two to research and target festivals from little to big, and map out a plan addressing their deadlines, entry costs, and mandates. Take into consideration the length of your finished product: it's easy to pop a six-minute short in front of anything, but much harder to find a spot for a sixty-eight-minute stand-alone piece that's not quite long enough to be a feature, but way too long to be a short. If your ultimate goal is a one-hour television broadcast, look at the actual guidelines for the venues you'll be approaching — whether PBS, cable, or traditional network channels — and determine your final cut's length accordingly.

If you're applying to a festival, you might be feeling some concern that it's a drawback for your piece to have been shot digitally. The politically correct response is that the power of the story is the one and only consideration for a film's success. The more complex truth is that because it's comparatively easy and inexpensive to complete a digital feature or short as opposed to one on film, the aggregate quality of digital submissions tends to be lower, or perceived as lower. This just means that your script, visuals, directing, and performances have to stand out even more; and if you've done your homework and found the right people to collaborate with, your image quality should be at a level where it doesn't stand between the viewer and the story.

Is it wise to submit a rough cut of your feature in the hopes of getting finishing funds? If you're thinking of "rough cut" as a barely coherent assembly of digital dailies in which only you and your mother can see the seeds of genius, then you'll be better served by waiting until the piece is in a much stronger form. However, if your story is truly compelling and the minor work left to be done will be accepted as a trade-off to factor into the purchase price and marketing costs, then yes. In other words, if the submission deadline is approaching and you know the piece can stand on its own merits even without the color corrections or final sound mix, then it's not unreasonable to enclose your current cut with your application, continue working on it, and then show up to the festival with a more polished version, which you then hope a distributor will be willing to put completion funding into as part of picking the movie up for release. For instance, *Tadpole* (starring Sigourney Weaver, John Ritter, and Bebe Newirth, and directed by Gary Winick, co-founder of InDigEnt) went to Sundance as a digital feature that was going to need a significant technical upgrade before it could be shown in theaters, and Miramax still bought the distribution rights for $5 million.   Unfortunately for digital enthusiasts, this charming coming-of-age comedy didn't give audiences the best possible impression of what digital image acquisition is currently capable of, and has consequently raised the bar for new digital features to prove themselves both aesthetically and at the box office.

David Schendel, director of *Yank Tanks*, is a firm believer in festivals, which helped get his documentary feature a theatrical distribution deal, as well as provide him with valuable experience: "Festivals are great to have your work seen and appreciated, especially when it's right out of the gate and you really don't know what people will think. The beauty of being a filmmaker is being able to sit in an audience with people seeing your film. That's when you learn, feeling the vibe and seeing what moves them and what doesn't. That's how you evolve as an artist." And another great thing about going to festivals is that whether you sell your film or not, you get producers coming up to you and saying they want to produce your next film. In fact, sometimes as soon as the movie is even accepted into a festival you'll have distributors calling you and asking for a screening copy (after all, distributors are trying to keep ahead of each other, as well). Also, press clippings, reviews, and audience responses at festivals are all things that distributors eat up.

Washington Heights, the urban Latino drama by first-time feature director Alfredo Rodriguez de Villa, eventually got a theatrical distribution deal solely because of its success at film festivals. The DV feature had no particular political connections and no big-name actors; people simply saw the film for what it was. Also, Alfredo knew going into the project that there was a very strong sub-genre of urban films for video marketing, and that he would probably make his money back on a video release if nothing else. But he even turned down a substantial straight-to-video offer because the feature was already racking up awards at festivals from Tribeca to Los Angeles to Austin to Milan.

From this highly favorable exposure, Alfredo took meetings from prospective distributors who varied in seriousness and financial offers, and the distributor who won the deal did so partly out of sheer persistence in courting the project. After the theatrical release in spring 2003, the film should be able to pay back its investors through a gradual release pattern, starting with Latino markets in New York, Miami, and other urban areas.

"Do not spend $2 million," Alfredo warns. "You will not get it back, and you will have a lot of pissed off people behind you." In other words, the fact that you get a first film out there is great, but don't spend two million unless you're going to get back 10. That's the rate of return you want. If you sell something that doesn't even get your negative cost back, you're working for free, and that doesn't make sense. Alfredo also advises against making something really commercial, since Hollywood is churning out, for instance, light romantic comedies all year long and that market is too flooded to let newcomers in, especially if your light romantic comedy isn't winning awards at festivals. Think carefully about the concept of your film, and think even harder about the economics. "I think it's bad for your career as a filmmaker to come in as the guy with debts. The guy who spends a lot of money and doesn't earn it back. But at the end of the day, if you can make money, they'll call you. No matter what the press says, or who thinks what, they'll call you."

THE WRAP

> If a movie is going to be successful with audiences, they first need to arrive at the conclusion that it is absolutely necessary for them to make time to go see it.

> The best way to convince audiences of this is through widespread word of mouth and through catching, or even becoming, the *zeitgeist* that sets the trend rather than follows it. The first happens when you have a good product that's effectively marketed to the right viewers. The second comes from plain luck and serendipity, so you're better off attending to the first.

> Festivals are still the best way for new filmmakers to get critical acclaim and public notice. Plus there's nothing to beat the learning experience or creative thrill of watching your movie in a theater with a live audience of strangers.

> Putting your digital movie on the Internet is a viable approach, but be aware of the loss of viewing quality that will happen with download time, image compression, and sound limitations.

Before undertaking the kind of commitment, labor, and expense it takes to pull off a digital project, you should ask yourself whether it's all going to be worth it to you if no one outside your immediate circle of friends and family ever sees the finished piece. Imagine that you spend all that time and money and get a couple of years older and deeper in debt, and still only a few people come to your one and only screening of the movie. Do you still believe that your story deserves to be told and that you're the one to tell it?

If so, then that's even more reason to make your movie than if you have an expectation or hope that it will someday be seen and applauded by a wide paying audience. Because the best reason to make movies is for the sake of the process and the story. If you're just cranking out product in pursuit of a paycheck, eventually you'll run out of things to sell. And if you're operating under self-imposed deadlines like "I'll give myself a year, or two years, or three years to use this movie to make myself rich and famous," then you're just giving yourself a timeline by which to fail.

The upside of pursuing moviemaking and storytelling purely for passion's sake is that the passion will show through. And that passion will help you take your movie to its ultimate objective, whether that's a private screening for your mom in her living room, the Grand Jury Prize at Sundance, or a giant distribution deal that allows you to retain your creative integrity while also buying that house in the hills. Hopefully, all three.

PART IV
A NEW
YEAR'S
RESOLUTION

chapter
thirteen

>>>*IT CAME FROM OUTER SPACE*

At some point in the foreseeable future, you might walk into a movie theater in a little town and sit down to watch a feature film that has been transmitted digitally to the theater's central server by way of a satellite broadcast. The content from the central server will then travel through high-speed data lines to the screening room that you're in, and be automatically uploaded and digitally projected for your viewing pleasure. No celluloid print, no FedEx truck to deliver the print, no printing costs for the studio that previously distributed the film (at around $1000 a print) to thousands of theaters. In this same happy world, the theater could be switching from feature to feature at different show times through an agreed-upon access system — again, no celluloid prints to get scratched or dirty, no restrictions on the geographic locations films could reach, no decrease in viewing quality over time. The technology to do all these things is out there. So what's the holdup? As usual: money.

Because the new equipment would be housed in, and immediately benefit, the theaters, the major studios are unwilling to pay for the pricey conversion of individual theaters from celluloid to digital projection. Meanwhile, theater owners, or exhibitors, stubbornly resist replacing perfectly good, low-maintenance, long-lasting, and relatively cheap (say $35,000 a unit versus $100,000 for a digital projector) film projectors when the long-term cost benefit is to the studios and other distributors who will no longer have to pay for prints and shipping. Not to mention the fact that many theater chains are going through drastic cost-cutting, bankruptcy, re-organization, or all three.

Another crucial issue is that current projectors are not as good as the industry wants them to be. But they'll get there, and the hope is that the standards created by Digital Cinema Initiatives (a joint effort by the seven major studios to establish guidelines for a cost-effective transition to digital projection) will set the bar very high in anticipation of new 4000-lines-of-resolution projection technology on the horizon. That way digital cameras, digital transmission, and the viewing experience will adapt upwards, rather than settling for the 2K resolution that is possible with today's hardware.

And digital projection is not as reliable as film, yet. Projectors need tweaking by highly paid technicians, color balances can slide, and if the machine isn't properly calibrated you'll be watching an image that isn't as rich in color or contrast as a beat-up film print on a thirty year-old projector. Even so, the politics of control of the technology — in other words, who between the distributors or the exhibitors will step up first — have slowed the advance of digital theaters much more than the technology itself, or even the financial considerations. Although the solutions to these issues may be a few years away, in the end what it will mean to storytellers everywhere is a greater freedom to share their visions.

A BRIEF LAYMAN'S DESCRIPTION OF THE MECHANICS OF DIGITAL PROJECTION

Currently, if you watch something digitally projected in a movie theater, chances are you're looking at images coming out of a Texas Instruments DLP projector, which is the most widespread technology for the moment. DLP stands for Digital Light Processing, and the light comes from a very bright bulb inside the digital projector. This lamp shines through a color wheel with red, green, and blue filters. The color-filtered light hits a semiconductor called a DMD (digital micro-mirror device) made up of as many as 1.3 million microscopic mirrors. Each of these mirrors corresponds to a single pixel that you will see on the theater screen, and each microscopic mirror tilts on a hinge in synchronization with the movement of the color wheel.

If the mirror is tilted toward the lamp (the "on" position), it reflects the lamp's light onto the screen as one pixel of the entire image. The color of each pixel is determined by how long the mirror is in the on position under which colors — to create a magenta pixel, for instance, the mirror is on under the red filter slightly longer than it is on under the blue filter, and it's tilted away (the "off" position) while light shines through the green filter. Your retina blends this mostly red-and-some-blue reflected speck of light, and sees a magenta pixel. Keep in mind that these mirrors are flipping back and forth thousands of times each second, so all that registers on your vision is seamless motion and natural-looking color gradations, assuming that everything is working properly.

There's a newer kind of projector called an LCOS (Liquid Crystal on Silicon), which offers higher resolution than a DLP projector and may eventually compete well against DLP projects, once its technology (based on JVC's Digital Direct Drive Image Light Amplifier, also known as D-ILA) matures. NTT is also coming out with a 4K projector (film resolution averages out at about 2000 lines, by comparison) that may set the bar for technical and creative standards. D-ILA images also start out with your basic fiercely bright lamp inside the projector. But the light shines through an LCD panel where the image is already playing in full color. Colored light comes through the LCD panel, bounces off the mirror, and out to the theater screen.[14] No microscopic mirrors, no color wheel, but its light level and dynamic contrast range have historically lagged those achieved by the DLP and, of course, analog film projection. Also, currently the D-ILA projector requires a technician to make monthly adjustments to its settings, and the DLP does not. (Neither do the old-fashioned film projectors.)

Either kind of digital projector can take digital images from a disc or tape master or a computer hard drive. If it's coming to a computer hard-drive, the idea down the road is for content owners to send material directly from one computer to another, by way of high-speed cable connections or, better yet, satellite transmissions. This raises significant piracy and access concerns, but once those issues are resolved, digital projection stands to offer big savings to the people who used

---

[14] "Get the Big Picture: Digital Projectors Bring Big Images To Homes & Businesses," *How Computers Work, Part II*, Winter 2002

to pay big bucks for film prints and shipping (namely, film distributors, who are usually studios, especially on the high-volume end of
distribution, such as when 3,000 film prints of *Terminator 3* arrive
simultaneously by way of traditional shipping methods at theaters all
over the country).

WILL EXHIBITORS STEP UP?

In fairness to the exhibitors, their industry is rising out of bankruptcy.
Theater owners don't want to pay for the new projectors, which still
cost upwards of $100,000 without providing either the resolution, reli-
ability, or longevity of the film projectors those same exhibitors paid
$30,000 or $40,000 for 10 to 20 years ago. Their hesitation is partially
justified by the fact that there still isn't a set standard for what kind of
resolution and quality these projectors are going to provide. In other
words, with a 4K projector soon to come, why would you invest millions of dollars in 2K projectors that won't satisfy your theater audiences, especially as those audiences start to get that same 2K level of
resolution from the spread of high-definition television sets in their
own homes?

As 4K projectors become available, in markets where ticket prices are
high, that kind of purchase decision can be more easily justified. Take
Japan, always a leader in technology, where movie tickets cost almost
$20 and audience members are numerous and dependable. And, a lot
of times the distributors in Japan also happen to be the owners of the
theater. So those companies can afford to install digital projectors,
and they have the incentive to do it, because they benefit from owning the hardware in the theaters, as well as saving the money on the
distribution side.

But in the United States, there's an inherent conflict of who is going to
pay for the retrofitting of theaters. Exhibitors want distributors to pay
for it, because exhibitors already have perfectly good film projectors,
and the distributors are the ones who will save money by eliminating
film printing and shipping costs. But the distributors don't want to
pay to upgrade somebody else's facility.

And yet, at least one major exhibitor looks ready to take the leap. Philip Anschutz owns Regal Entertainment, the largest movie theater chain in the country, after Anschutz acquired and merged Regal Cinemas, United Artists, and Edwards Cinemas. This puts him in charge of almost 20% of the nation's movie screens (the total number is in the high thirty-thousands, even with continuing theater closures), and he has plans to use nearly 80% of those locations as a testing ground for digital projection. By the end of 2003, Regal Entertainment intends to retrofit those theaters with digital projectors, high-speed data networking equipment, and satellite links.

The company will start recouping this $70 million investment by digitally projecting advertisements before the main event, and will also be using the equipment to project digital short programs generated through Regal's agreement with NBC. Gradually, the Regal theaters will plug in high-end hardware upgrades to enable the projection of digital features, as standards and technology stabilize. Once those elements fall into place, the strategy goes, Regal will be far ahead of the competition in having the infrastructure and business partners to make it a leader in the digital future of movie theaters.[15]

WILL THE DISTRIBUTORS STEP UP?
The studios have protested loudly at the notion of paying for equipment to be located in somebody else's building. Imagine your neighbor asking you to buy him a new washer and dryer (even if you got a percentage of his laundry revenues). The studios also point out that exhibitors will get to use digital projectors for all kinds of other events that the distributors won't get a piece of. But the truth is that the studios are going to be the ones to save the most money when digital projection becomes the norm.

It also won't necessarily be the major studios who see the most benefit. At Lions Gate Films, right now, on a wide release, they spend somewhere around $10 million doing it. Published figures from the MPAA indicate that when the major studios (Fox, Disney, Paramount,

---

[15]"Regal is Ready for Its Digital Close-Up," P.J. Huffstutter, *Los Angeles Times*, December 4, 2002

Warner Bros., and Universal) go out wide, they spend on average $30 million marketing the motion pictures. But the cost of making the prints remains about the same. So if Lions Gate is making 1000 prints at $1000 a pop, that's a million dollars, and it's the same fixed cost for the major studios. This means that if you eliminated the need to make and pay for these prints, Universal saves $1 million out of $30 million, but Lions Gate saves $1 million out of $10 million — a 3% savings versus a 10% savings.

By the above math, proportionately, the changeover to digital transmission and projection will benefit smaller distributors just as much or more than it will big ones. Anytime there's new technology, it can help smaller entrepreneurial companies get past the barriers-to-entry a little more easily. The other side of that, though, is that whoever controls the new technology is usually the same guy who controls the old technology, and they'll still try to make the same profit from you as they did before. But for smaller distributors who live and die by their profit margin in a way that vast conglomerates don't, digital projection surely provides the possibility of critical breathing space.

Despite all these revisionist business models brewing, no one is going to go for it until it's proven itself to be a superior delivery system to the one in place before. That's where the technology itself comes in.

WHERE THE TECHNOLOGY SITS
Ironically, digital projection is far more ready for primetime than digital image capture, although there has been a decline in both studio and exhibitor interest in it. At one point, there were predictions of having a thousand digital screens by the end of 2002, and instead maybe 60 or 70 had come into play. There is a lot of support for digital projection of images captured on film. But right now, the Texas Instrument DLP only offers audiences 1280 x 1024 lines of resolution. JVC's D-ILA is based on a less mature technology. Neither has the dynamic contrast range of film projection. Also, if you're projecting at the 2K resolution of HDTV, you have to be three picture heights away to not

see the pixels. Most stadium seating theaters are a maximum of three-and-a-half pictures heights deep. So HDTV-quality theaters won't be good enough for most people not to see the pixels.

But wait; there's hope. The 4000-lines-of-resolution projector being developed by NTT looks, according to industry witnesses, unbelievable. 4K actually offers four-times the resolution of a 2K projector because it's a two-dimensional upgrade, and soon manufacturers might reach a tilting point where the cost of a 4K projector becomes competitive with that of a film projector. Right now, prices aren't even close. And the costs of printing celluloid, while still substantial, aren't as prohibitive as a full-fledged entry into digital projection would be at current market prices. First of all, what studios pay for release prints isn't the book-list quote from the film lab. When studios sign a contract with a film lab, they are advanced a check for tens of thousands of dollars, which they gradually apply against future orders, so in reality they're paying a lot less than $1000 for a print. Compare the cost of $12,000 to run your studio's prints in a theater for a year, to $100,000 just to buy a projector. Then add on the price of the accompanying hardware conversion at anywhere from $2000 to $20,000 per site, and you see why technology prices have a long way to come down.

And this kind of decision is going happen when it's a no-brainer decision to make. When VCRs came out, they were $700, and it was a big commitment to be one of the first consumers to purchase one. Now you can get a DVD player for $95, and you hardly have anything to lose by trying one out. If they had sold the first thousand Texas Instruments projectors for $40,000 and taken an initial loss in return for securing a hold on the market, we wouldn't even be talking about this now. But it's good they didn't, because now 4K resolution digital projectors are coming out, and the initial frenzy has quieted to the point where the industry is more careful about what it embraces. Since movie distributors don't want to be in an unfavorable competition against a higher resolution available at home on HDTV, they're willing to wait a little longer and make sure that digital cinema has a standard, probably 4000 lines of resolution, that not only satisfies audiences and content creators, but fills theater seats. The current attitude from Digital Cinema Initiatives seems to be that if they're going to do this correctly, they need to set the bar high, trust that the technology will keep pace, and thereby expand the creative palette, instead of limiting it.

The advantages of digital projection are not just lines of resolution and knee-jerk techo-admiration, either. Look at the way celluloid comes to audiences now. In normal printing from a film negative, you make a contact inter-positive and you lose resolution. You then make a contact inter-negative and again you lose some resolution. Then the release prints race off the machines at 3000 feet a minute, and you lose resolution again. Then, when the film is projected, the heat blisters out as it's moving through the gate, so it's not actually as in-focus as it should be.

One of the attractions for cinematographers is that digital projection offers a significant enhancement in the consistency of image quality. Theoretically, everyone sees the same image projected because there are no degradations of celluloid prints. Sometimes in a movie theater, the lamps are turned down to a lower power consumption level so that the life of the projection xenon lamp will be extended, and this lowers the viewing quality of the print. Moreover, modern projectors have a tower system, which puts 2000-foot rolls into one large loop, and handling of the print can cause damage from scratching and dirt. Also, a lot of ultraviolet light impacts the film print as it's exposed to the xenon lamps in the projector; sustained exposure to this UV light can fade the color on the film print.

With good contrast and color reproduction, digital projection can look much better than film projection. If you're doing post-production on a digital intermediate (a digitized version of whatever footage you originally shot), at the end of the process audiences are seeing the material closer to its original source, and everyone theoretically can see an answer print quality, which they don't see now (you see release prints in the theaters, which are essentially copies of copies).

At any rate, before anyone can proceed with widespread retrofitting of theaters for digital projection, the technology has to stabilize to a standardized level of resolution quality. Secondly, the cost of manufacturing the projectors has to hit a point where it makes sense for people to buy them, which means dipping well below the $100,000 mark. In addition, the reliability factor of technical operation standards has to be almost flawless, and it needs to be able to withstand a lot of wear and tear. On top of that, there's the debate over how access is granted to this content, and what safeguards there are against piracy. Distributors will want to control when and where their digital movies are shown, but exhibitors will want a fair solution that doesn't burden them with the cost of supporting the digital rights management technology.

Once those costs and specifications are agreed on, the distributors and exhibitors might still, sensibly, want to look for alternatives to sinking billions of their own dollars into capital improvements. They may look for cash sources off balance sheet, in other words, for money in structures from outside financiers. To those outside financiers, distributors and exhibitors could offer a piece of the revenue that is generated by digital distribution and projection, perhaps structuring the deal so that the percentages of those profits shift as the new equipment starts to pay for itself and depreciate in value over time. Even with the cost of new security systems to protect against piracy, and all the other technological necessities, distribution stands to have the lion's share of savings from not making and shipping prints anymore.

CONTENT FROM OUTSIDE OF HOLLYWOOD AND THE INDEPENDENT SCENE

Here's a novel thought: distributing digital content that is not a feature film, and offering exhibitors and audiences alternative content and entertainment that expressly has nothing to do with traditional Hollywood creations. Boeing Digital Cinema has been very active and innovative in this area, and also comes equipped with its own satellite connectivity. Through proprietary technology, they can provide concerts and sporting events with very high quality, high-definition transmissions. Similarly, "WorldStage" is an alternative entertainment company that sprang out of Video Applications, Inc., a staging and rental business that typically works with corporate clients from CBS to Porsche on live presentations with digitally projected, ultra-high-definition (1024 x 3840 lines of resolution) components.

The company has developed a plan to deliver content — such as concerts, sports, holiday shows, business to business corporate programs, and educational programs — to theater exhibitors without dealing with Hollywood or independent distributors at all. In its anticipated roll-out, WorldStage will take over a screen (from projector installation to maintenance and content delivery) full time in an existing multiplex, and support new programming with VAI's own digital network. Ultimately, they intend to provide affordable satellite transmission of the digital content to the theaters, and they'll have a digital rights management aspect to make those transmissions secure. So, in a population center of the right target size, parents could drop their teens off at the local multiplex to watch a live rock concert in a familiar, controlled environment, go watch a movie themselves in the meantime, and then meet up with the kids afterwards.

And it's not just like watching a film of a rock concert, either. In the WorldStage theater lab in Tustin, California, you sit down in front of an 'N Sync concert that was captured on high-definition video and mixed in Dolby 5.1 Surround Sound. The screams of young girls fill the air as the lights dim; the members of the boy band go into action on the theater-sized screen, singing and dancing in their usual manner, accompanied by clouds of dry ice and a whizzing light show inside the screening room, all synchronized with the lights on the live stage and the pounding music from the concert performance. The sound system shakes our chairs with the roar of the crowd, and it's easy to imagine being in a packed theater and applauding for what feels like a live performance.

WHAT DOES ALL THIS MEAN TO YOU?

Eventually, film projection will be obsolete. And there'll be a few prints left for those stubborn theaters that have old projectors. But with digital projection the accepted norm, and in getting a rock-solid image that is perfect quality without any grain, are we actually getting a better image? Many think that the steadier, cleaner, more highly resolved, consistently brighter image is necessarily better. The film image, created by a beam of light through moving celluloid, has a jitter and a wave in the focus. Those things breathe a little bit of life into the film, giving it randomness and beauty, which digital would have to spend a ton of money to emulate with a computer program. So a certain visual poetry will be gone forever. Then again, plenty of people (recalling Neil Young's famous essay) think that CDs don't sound as good as vinyl, but that doesn't mean the industry didn't switch over. Eventually resolutions will match and the human eye won't see the difference between digital and film projection, and new audiences won't miss what they never knew — the same way that most modern audiences have never seen old silver halide prints shimmering on the truly silver screen. From that point of view, progress is not always better, just more efficient.

Well, onward and upward. The way things have traditionally worked, a smaller film like *The Guys* gradually moves into more theaters while a wide release like *The Hulk* is slowly dropping back week-by-week. Imagine you're an independent distributor and you could send a video of *The Guys* out — digitally or otherwise — telling theater owners in distant locations that this movie really has legs and will appeal to your audiences right now, and why make them wait a couple of months before they can see it? Maybe some theater owner in Madison, Wisconsin is willing to put your movie on one of her screens because she can make that decision by just pushing a button to accept satellite delivery. In that scenario, neither the exhibitor nor the distributor has to make an expensive decision before getting to the audience. Take *The Blair Witch Project*, which needed four or five weeks to physically make prints to catch up with the wildfire demand from audiences; unexpected hits like that could take hold and reach audiences much more quickly. Right now the biggest filter between the film and the audience is not the critics but the marketing campaigns. When digital transmission and projection is in place, critics and audiences might have more influence over the demand and the flow of what they see.

Eliminating the cost of prints also means that, if the conglomerates don't stand in the way, independents may have more of a shot at distribution throughout the country. Especially if, for example, you put BMWs in your film and then BMW pays for the advertising costs (doesn't sound too independent, but hey, it gets your movie made).

THE WRAP

> Digital projectors don't give audiences the resolution or reliability of film projectors yet, but 4K projection promises to be the new standard.

> When the cost of digital projectors sinks and the quality of the digital image rises to the point where audiences will buy enough tickets to make money for the owners of the hardware, digital projection systems will become the norm in theaters.

> Independent moviemakers and non-Hollywood content distributors both stand to benefit from advances in digital projection. Whether through new art-house circuits or alternatives to narrative fare, more content holders than ever will be able to reach far-flung, self-selected audiences.

Whatever new kinds of partnerships come into being to address new distribution and financing methods, digital filmmakers won't have to pay for the steps of film printing, shipping, or possibly even advertising, if the audience wants the movie; you could go directly from the digital image to the projection of it. There could be a digital film circuit, with quick turnovers and movies going on to new theaters in quick succession. This kind of art house DV circuit wouldn't incur tremendous costs to distribute those independent digital movies, and the biggest beneficiary of that would be the audiences and the storytellers — you.

chapter
fourteen

>>>*SEND IN THE CLONES*

George Lucas has been at the forefront of digital cinema as both a vocal proponent of the technological change underway and a driving force in shaping and accelerating that change. For *Episode II: Attack of the Clones*, Lucas used a camera developed at his direct request: the CineAlta 24P from Sony, which shoots at film-standard 24fps, rather that at video's 30fps norm. Sony is a logical developer of digital hardware from cameras to interactive television systems, since its studio is vertically integrated from technological innovation to film production to multimedia distribution. However, it is not alone in the field. Other research-and-development leaders are those with the most to gain from a successful digital transition. Continuing advances in digital effects and "pipelines," or Internet interfaces are enabling production, special effects, and editing teams to work together for a fraction of the turnaround-time and costs incurred by an all-film post.

At the same time, one of the side effects of digital possibilities has been the development of a certain techno-lust, an adoration and advocacy of technology for its own sake. There's something about technology that goes into the human psyche, and that lends itself to the enthusiasm of people who are single-mindedly bent on replacing film with digital formats. Sometimes the people who push those views are pushing their company's products, so be sure to put any grand proclamations about the supremacy of digital into the context of what the speaker or the speaker's company has to gain by promoting that belief. We personally believe that digital is, on the whole, a terrific and accessible tool, but to oversimplify its current condition and its promise would be to overlook its complexities and its place in the context of the past and the future. To take two sobering hype-versus-reality checks as an example:

1. All "HDTV-ready" means is that the television set will accept the HDTV signal. Some models will then simply reduce that gorgeous high definition down to the 720 lines of resolution physically available on that particular lower-end monitor.

2. Footage from the Sony 24P HD camera, versus the Sony F950, versus the Thompson Viper camera, still will not measure up to a competing test of 35-millimeter film footage that was sampled at 4000 lines of resolution, down-rezzed to 2000 lines and then projected on the same 1.3K digital projector as the digitally acquired images were.

Okay, fine, so film still looks better, and a real 1920-line HDTV monitor really is too expensive for the average person to get right now. These inequities won't stay the same forever, since companies are still involved in research and development and profits. But research costs money, and the film industry, especially the big business side, has never been as conservative as it is right now. So the idea of investing in an unproven technology before it'll pay off is not an exciting one to any studio, as it scrutinizes its ledgers, quarter to quarter, between investment and returns.

POST-PRODUCTION PIONEERS
Fortunately for all of us, we don't have to rely only on studio budgets to get research and development done. For instance, IBM and CNN are working on a new interconnected global system for field reporters, central production, and broadcasting stations to work together with suppliers around the world in acquiring, storing, and accessing news content digitally. They'll provide material in high resolution for broadcast, low resolution for Web browsers, and in the form of metadata so that people can research a database-type archive by all kinds of key elements, such as date aired, story subject, and images filmed.

As other technology companies are also finding, it's in IBM's interest to help the technology and management side of digital creation and distribution become transparent. To this end, they have fostered open operating platforms and workstations based on free Linux code (instead of proprietary software programs whose creators charge users for access). In the post-production world, this allows digital artists to share information and files, and concentrate on creating content, more cheaply and more quickly. At Weta in New Zealand, Linux Intellistations allowed visual effects teams to move massive quantities of data around easily while working on shots for *The Lord of the Rings* trilogy. Because the artists can do their work better and faster, it enhances the marketable momentum of a creative community, and everybody wins. Furthermore, IBM's next step is to make the technology self-serving — in other words, to design an infrastructure that can manage itself through autonomic computing. IBM predicts that this technological workload will take care of itself within the next two to three years.

Post-production, with its tight turnaround schedules, data volume and creative pressures, is immediately benefiting from the speed and flexibility of digital pipelines. Digital Fountain delivers digital dailies via the Internet, much faster than would be possible by traditional methods. In six hours, Digital Fountain can transfer telecined dailies from Burbank to Miami (faster than flying an overnight courier) in a perfect, reliable and securely transmitted copy. Better yet, both sides can keep their existing T1 or DSL connectivity system. This allows for a quick review and approval cycle, and quick access to content by remote post-production facilities.

Even fancier in its offerings is ShowRunner, which implements a converged digital network using geostationary satellites. Once you pay for a package of services, you can choose to share the type of data and images you want to exchange with other people. For instance, a nomadic director shooting around the world could be showing dailies and providing other information to studio executives in Los Angeles. Warner Bros., Paramount, and Dreamworks are some of the clients taking advantage of ShowRunner's real-time collaboration services for

editing, teleconferencing, and decision-making among multiple locations. Now that satellite technology has become both more affordable
and more powerful, ShowRunner can transmit this interactive capability on demand, wherever it is needed, over high-speed wireless links,
in the form of data that is securely encrypted. Founder Curtis Clark
believes that ShowRunner will save money and also lead to the making of better films; the system is designed to mesh with the current
workflow model in the industry, and not to change it.[16]

DIGITAL ASSET MANAGEMENT: NECESSITY OR MYTH?

So there's all this digital information floating around. Digitally
acquired images, content, and elements either working on hard drives,
archived elsewhere, or zipping back and forth on pipelines and networks. How are we going to keep track of it all? First, just the logistical side: digital asset management.

Digital asset management follows the same principles as using data-
bases to manage large quantities of information, but it's much more
complex and interactive. Unfortunately, just to take an example
from the film industry, there's no uniformity among the users
inputting descriptions of data: M & E versus Music and Effects versus music-and-effects, and so on. The human factor is definitely the
weakest link in managing all the digital data out there. The interaction of people, their transience in a job, and most of all, their
inexactness in communicating with the technology, is where the
system breaks down. So the unfortunate truth is that, at the
moment, digital asset management makes things more complicated, harder to deal with later on, more expensive, and less interop-
erable. Furthermore, there is no such thing as a digital archive with
indefinite value as a source of record-keeping and preservation.
Everyone agrees that digital archiving formats keep getting better,
so the proposed solution is data migration from format to format,
as technology advances. The idea is that every three to five years,
you take everything and copy it over. One result of this is that you
have 50 computer people managing the creative content of four

---

[16]Detailed specifications are available at *www.netune.com*

people. But new versions of technology are very often not backward compatible, and none of this is standardized.

The other problem is, forget about software upgrades and human error. Think back to the very first personal computers, which were considered spiffy if they had a 64K operating hard drive. Assuming people kept their TRS-80s intact, to get at the information stored inside them today, they'd need to find someone with a working reader and a 5 1/2" disk. Digital video equipment is less plagued by this kind of obsolescence than digital audio because it's such an effort to create a new line of products. But how long can you guarantee that a certain kind of video playback deck is going to be around? Even if you make a point of buying extra machines so that you don't have to worry about finding parts for them 20 years down the line, in 20 years how many people are going to be able to operate those machines?

This brings us back to the standards issue, and the expectation is that once the industry adopts a firm stance on a format and lines of resolution, then product will be stored on that, and also, ironically, on film. It's kind of like printing out your files on paper so that you can be absolutely sure you have the content in an easily and universally accessible form, no matter what. Sometimes there's just no substitute for the analog solution.

DIGITAL RIGHTS MANAGEMENT

As with most systems that determine who gets to make money on a thing, there's a certain urgency to digital rights management development (DRM) development and implementation. DRM deals with any technology controlling access to, copying, or distribution of digital content. Consequently, these efforts address standards of hardware, as well as changes in software copyright law. So if an asset owner (such as Warner Bros.) transmits content (the first *Batman* movie) to the user (you, watching digital TV on your couch), a DRM system will enforce the conditions for access established by the asset owner, and gives usage data to the asset owner. In other words, depending on the usage agreement, you might be paying a monthly fee to watch that digital television, and Warner Bros. gets to find out how many television sets are tuning into its programming every day. The basic goal of DRM is to create a reliable system for controlling and tracking content distribution and access via a "black box" of controls, whether this black box is physical hardware or software encryption programs.

Currently, there's no single standardized method for digital rights management, though there are various competing proprietary systems, some of which are patented. Also, there is no perfectly secure system to stop people from gaining unauthorized access to view and possibly pirate digital product. In addition to the technological intricacies involved, there's a need to balance the interests of competing groups. Creators want access and revenue; distributors, technology providers, and retailers want the DRM to be non-proprietary (so that there's only one standardized version of whatever this solution is), something that can interface with existing systems, something that supports different business models, and something that is easy to implement. Consumers, including schools and researchers, want something that is easy to use, reasonably priced, and allows for fair use and personal use. (Fair uses include research, educational purposes, commentary, parodies, and so forth.)

The Digital Millennium Copyright Act, signed into law in 1998, prohibits circumventions of access and copy control technologies. According to the DMCA, you can't break the encoding on a DVD of *Star Wars* and then sell copies over the Internet; you can't come up with a method to break the encoding; in fact, you can't even present a paper at a scientific conference or in another public venue and discuss what you know about someone else's method of bypassing the copy-protection feature on a DVD.[17]

What about tangible enforcement of those principles? The Consumer Broadband and Digital Television Promotion Act was proposed in

---

[17]"Unintended Consequences: Three Years Under the DMCA," Electronic Frontier Foundation Whitepaper, 2002

Congress in the spring of 2002 by Senator Fritz Hollings, the chairman of the Senate Commerce Committee. If passed into law, this would create mandatory DRM by requiring that any kind of software or hardware that reproduces, displays, accesses, or retrieves any kind of copyrighted work also be designed to automatically block unauthorized copying of those copyrighted works. The ideas in the legislation are backed by the entertainment industry, and are intended to ensure the secure transmission of copyrighted content. So film distributors and record companies would attach digital tags to their products with encoded rules about how those movies and songs could be played, viewed, copied, or distributed on digital TVs, personal computers, and MP3 players. It would be illegal to remove these tags and illegal to circumvent their restrictions by any means. If, after one year of the new law being in effect, manufacturers and content owners can't settle on a single security system to enforce these measures, the Federal Communications Commission can step in to make its own regulations for the matter.[18]

The idea is for content owners to be able to control use, but for end users to maintain fair access. The bill's supporters claim that regulations and the technology to enforce them will actually benefit consumers by making content providers more comfortable with, for instance, showing movies on the Internet once they're confident that no one can pirate them. But opponents of the bill, such as *DigitalConsumer.org*, worry that it would give the entertainment industry control over both new technology and consumers' rights, even though Senator Hollings has given public assurances that people will still be able to make legitimate consumer copies of programming in their own homes.[19] In a way, the conflict comes down to the opposition between Silicon Valley and Hollywood. The first wants to let market forces, consumers, and technology gradually settle on workable fair use practices, and the second has repeatedly asked the government to step in and actively prevent piracy.

---

[18]"Anti-Copy Bill Hits D.C.," Declan McCullagh, *Wired News*, March 22, 2002

[19]"Hollings Proposes Copyright Defense," Mike Musgrove, *Washington Post*, March 22, 2002

Again with the big bad studios. Are they trying to get unfair control of copyright and content access? More reasonable is the assumption that content controllers (which include you with your freshly shot digital movie) just want to be fairly compensated. The consumer demand for ease of access at a fair price led to the Napsterization of the music industry, and there are arguments that if record labels had been more sensitive to the needs of consumers from the start — by making their prices more reasonable to begin with, or by participating in efforts to share music on the Internet instead of vehemently standing in the way — they could have headed off some of that piracy. With that lesson now in the collective consciousness, it's up to studios to take advantage of the available consumer market. They can't put their heads in the sand and pretend that the demand and the technological capabilities aren't out there; they've got to figure out smart ways to provide consumers with what they want.

To that end, companies like MacroVision are developing solutions to protect the distribution of digital products. When a movie is sent out digitally over a network from a studio to a digital theater, or to a producer watching dailies in a remote location, the MacroSAFE ecosystem limits the use of that product to what the content creator intends. The technology comes in three parts:

1. A packager, or software tool, encrypts the digital product in an mpeg2 stream. So now your digital film travels in a form that is completely, but methodically, scrambled via an algorithm written in open-source computer code. Think of this packager as a code machine that takes a normal sentence, mixes up all the letters into nonsense, and then transmits the nonsense.

2. A receiver on the client end has a key to open this encrypted digital information, unscramble it, and present it for viewing as if nothing ever happened. So you as the client on the receiving end have the key to the code, and after using this key you can put the nonsense letters back in their original

form and read the sentence that was sent to you. It's much more complex than that, but that's the effect. The MacroSAFE receiver allows a client to review the transmitted material, but not to make changes or pass it on to someone else. It's basically a software viewer.

3. MacroVision provides a DRM server between these two things. When the content owner gives the DRM server the go-ahead, the DRM server sends out a licensing and encryption key to the client. The client (whether a theater or a private party) reinforces the usage rules established by the content owner.

Although MacroVision generally uses MacroSAFE for projects on the studio level or from other major Hollywood production houses, this kind of technology is also applicable to consumer-based movie distribution over the Internet. Say you have a digital movie that you want to broadcast over the Internet; you want to charge a viewing fee, and you don't want viewers to be able to randomly copy and re-send your movie. Certain products from Microsoft are designed for the consumer level, but you're supposed to use Windows Media for the format. If you use a Microsoft product to protect your content from being pirated, the viewing fee part will still be processed by an e-commerce site, such as PayPal, that is already set up to process credit cards and so forth. The protection software also has nothing to do with driving traffic to you, so in addition to the e-commerce site to process the credit cards, you might want to link yourself to other places where independent filmmakers or likely audience members already go.

Thus, as software and hardware developers counter what the market demands, we'll have more flexible technology that allows fair uses and a wide variety of ways to offer them; the technology will support the decisions of consumers and businesses, instead of restricting them.

The intent of content protection is to keep honest people honest, which can be accomplished by making the protection transparent, so it doesn't interfere with normal use, and so consumers can get the access they want without feeling like they're being unfairly regulated or punished for the activities of a few bad apples. Then you go up the threat chain to highly skilled pirates with lots of tools and large financial incentives to hack into these content protection systems. The key is having an effective way to patch holes if and when a security breach happens during the distribution process. It's very important that the protection system is flexible enough to respond to individual attacks and be patched up in an ongoing way — not like the Enigma code in World War II (once the Allies broke the code, it stayed broken, much to the detriment of the Nazis still using the code). Patching the protection system as you go would mean that only one week's material might become vulnerable, for instance, but then once the thing was repaired, you could continue using it without throwing the whole system out the window.

DRM technology has already come into play on a consumer level with Movielink, which offers viewers video-on-demand in a joint venture with Warner Bros., Paramount, Universal, MGM, and Sony. From the comfort of your home computer, you can visit the Web site and download easily as many titles as are available in your local video chain store, for comparable fees of $1.99 to $3.99. After you download Movielink Manager software to control your access, the movie arrives on your hard drive (that download takes an hour or so if you've got DSL), it will hang around for up to 30 days while you wait for an opportunity to watch it. Once you choose to play the movie, you have a 24-hour window to watch the movie as many times as you want. After that 24 hours, poof, it's gone, but at least you don't have to worry about a late return fee, or even being kind and rewinding.

In a way, this is a chance for the studios to throw consumers a bone — the theory goes that if they dissipate our pent-up need for movies, we won't feel such a need for piracy. Does it mean that the Internet as a distribution vehicle is finally going to make the breakthrough that everyone keeps anticipating? The answer as usual is: maybe, eventually. For Movielink, the studios set their own pricing, license films on a non-exclusive basis (meaning that they can also keep showing films in all the other places they're normally shown), and pick their own schedules for when they allow the content to be seen. Movielink claims to be going about its services a smarter way than the late and fairly unlamented Intertainer, which shut down after its streaming-entertainment-via-monthly-subscription model failed to keep the site alive. In contrast, Movielink operates on a transaction-to-transaction basis, and hopes to appeal to a younger (i.e., bored and awake at 2 a.m.) crowd and also people who could enjoy carrying movies around on their laptops: commuters, parents with kids in the car (no sense talking to them), and so on.

Movielink uses Real and Microsoft DRM technology, and as a result, also uses their media players as well.[20] Along with CinemaNow and MovieFlix (similar in setup to Movielink, though MovieFlix also offers movies via a monthly subscription service), this site is looking at an audience of PC users with cable modems and DSL. Five years down the line, though, around the same time they hope to be turning their first profits, they all want to be expanding into networked homes, which by then ought to be equipped with home servers that can acquire content from the Internet and send it to an appropriate display device, such as a digital TV or a bedroom computer monitor.

THE WRAP

> Digital post-production pipelines are becoming part of the infrastructure of the entertainment industry. Flexibility and invisibility help integrate digital technology into the creative process through offering filmmakers and their teams speedy collaboration wherever they are in the world.

> Digital rights management is steadily becoming more transparent and widespread, since the security of copyrighted content can be directly translated into money.

---

[20]"Movielink's CEO Speaks as the Studios Finally Make Their Big Jump Online," *www.VentureReporter.net*, November 18, 2002

> Due to limitations in home computers' capabilities to down-
load and play movies, and because studios are starting to provide affordable moviewatching experiences via the Internet,
it's much less likely that the film industry will experience the
same Napsterization that the music industry did.

It all sounds very Jetsons, but it's not such a stretch from TiVo and
DirecTV — or is it? The thing is that those systems operate off of analog broadcast towers for the most part (and require your television to
have its own digital satellite receiver), and the conversion of all of the
world's television signals to digital is another piece of the puzzle in
determining how long it will take before we are just that cool. Right
now, many local television stations don't have the capability to re-
broadcast digital signals that are being sent to them via satellite or
over-the-air (transmitting tower to transmitting tower). Estimates for
the cost of the average analog station to totally upgrade its receiving
and transmitting capabilities to digital standards are in the ballpark of
$3 million. The FCC is pushing for a transition to digital television to
be substantially accomplished by the end of 2006, but this goal might
be optimistic in the light of upgrade costs and market pressures
against conversion. Then again, one of the things about change is
that the speed of that change keeps getting faster and faster. People
got robot dogs for the holidays last year; who's to say what we can
ask for next?

chapter
fifteen

>>>*SIGNAL IN A BOTTLE*

In the mid-1980s, many people weren't sure what a CD player was. By 1990, most people had never sent an e-mail. And just before the millennium, few would have called digital video a vital media influence. What developments can we expect to see in the ensuing years?

Two things have been true about the progress of technology in general: it becomes more capable as it becomes more affordable, and the speed of its change increases exponentially over time (Moore's Law states this). Between now and when today's kindergarteners are graduating from college, three major areas are likely to have the most impact in what movie audiences watch and how they watch it: digital projection, digital television, and Internet delivery. Hardware for the first two already exists. The question of who will pay for theater conversion costs will be resolved as profit and survival incentives increase, and the initially slow consumer response to home digital TV systems such as TiVo is already changing significantly. As for the Internet, streaming video capabilities remain limited, but the speed and quality of video viewing via the Internet is constantly improving. Once home computer users start to connect to the Internet over cable rather than phone lines, and as public access to computers increases, filmmakers may find entirely new audiences for works that previously would have been undistributed in conventional venues.

DIGITAL TELEVISION
The process of changing over terrestrial broadcasting (regular broadcast stations) to digital transmission is going very slowly. The FCC may get involved in establishing "broadcast flag" technology that will be incorporated into television, computer, and other consumer electronics to prevent pirating of digital content. Hollywood supports this for

copyright protection reasons, but many technology providers believe that the realistic threat of Napsterization of digital content doesn't exist due to the technological constraints on end users and the computer and home theater equipment out there today. The question of whether copyright protection enforcement is holding back progress, like many of the dilemmas of emerging digital technologies, will likely settle out once profits and technological performance outweigh other downsides.

Digital television transmission doesn't necessarily mean that you're getting high-definition programs. High-definition digital TV looks much, much better than standard definition TV, and in the next several years as consumers replace their obsolete analog TVs with digital ones, and as the prices of high-end HD models drop, viewers will be inclined to use and show off the equipment to its best advantage. The gradual changeover to digital TV means that there will be a new window opening for the creation of digital product, because when the television industry switches to digital and high-definition content, TV libraries that were created and mastered on tape (as opposed to film, assuming you have all the various elements necessary for digital remastering) won't match the image quality of newer programming, and will therefore sink in value. In that sense, shooting on HD will give your product broadcast longevity down the road.

You might even be able to broadcast it in 3-D, if the efforts of companies like Cobalt Entertainment pan out. 3-D high-definition now boasts cameras that can be maneuvered easily to capture sports and other high-octane events that take voyeurism to the next level. We saw a test of Cobalt's technology, and quickly forgot we were wearing those little paper eyeglasses when crystal clear skateboarders and football players started running around and sailing out toward us. It was like peering into a jewel-like world of miniature people you could reach out and touch. Designed to be the visual equivalent of Dolby 5.1 surround sound, this science-fiction-esque technology might be in your living room sooner than you think.

More immediately, the impact of digital TV will lower the barriers to entry for smaller companies that are looking to enter the broadcast world. Even so, the success of those companies will still come down to the creative product. The true bottom line will be whether they can tell a compelling story with people that audience wants to see. In the end, it's never about the delivery mechanism. It's always about the package, the bundling of story, characters and audience appeal — in other words, what you're creating for an audience, and not how you're getting it in front of them.

WILL WE EVER NOT NEED FILM AT ALL?
If most theatrical features go to high-definition and digital projection in the future, then film will become kind of a niche material, just as is happening slowly in the world of professional still photography. Following the pattern of personal computers, digital hardware products continue to have more speed, more capacity, and lower prices, whereas film processes and prices haven't changed very much over the years.

The dynamic color range of DV is still very different from that of film, and color-space is now an issue — on set, you're concerned with whether your digital camera is capturing reds as reds and greens as greens; as you try to get the look you want, adjusting the green control affects the red or blue of everything else. Because of the way digital cameras are set up, the image is now tuned with electronics and not with chemistry or filters. In some ways it's more dangerous, but in other ways, if you have a technical understanding, it's very freeing. The challenge for the next digital generation is to use the knowledge of digital's capabilities more, in terms of special effects and color and pushing the envelope of what a film looks like. It's only a matter of time before some real geniuses start to use this palette in new ways, even if up until now, the focus has just been getting, for less money, a movie on the table.

Will film ever be totally obsolete? Probably not. We used to have just chemical labs, and now we have digital labs that work with chemical labs. Eventually color correction and effects and post will all happen on a digital intermediate, and then every film will be mastered in several different platforms to accommodate both film and digital projection. Because major films will still be archived on film. Let's say hypothetically in 20 years, 80% of the theaters in the United States have digital projection. Even in a case where you make a film solely for the American market, there will be a museum market, and a need for archiving. Digital projectors are changing every year. Until this industry settles down, which may take 20 years, you need that capacity to have a permanent record. Take an old film projector and hit it with a hammer, and you can fix it. This is not the case with current digital projectors. That's why film's going to be important, and why museums are going to want film: so that things don't get lost.

THE INTERNET
In the meantime, the Internet is the ultimate fire for us cave dwellers to gather around and hear a new story every night. The immediacy and economy of digital allows you to grab an image, plug it into the computer, see the pictures, and send as many pictures as you want to as many people in the world over the Internet. Even if you don't make a dime off your movies, creative synergies can spark off of finding other people out there. J. C. Calciano ran an Internet film festival called Webdance, and he had kids sending him "these great little films. And they would say to me, meeting you over the Internet inspired me. I'm going to make one film a month now. And they did, and you could see the progress of their craft and their storytelling."

Film has really replaced novels, and also talking about the weather. You meet somebody at a party, and *Have you seen any good movies lately?* is such a basic question. When the exchange of digital movies is really going to change things is when the Internet delivery medium reaches a global broadband. For instance, the music industry is coming to the point where 10 or 15 years from now, there may not be record companies controlling distribution so closely, because people will be able to get music on the Internet and via digital radio. If that same power ever happens with films, it truly will be a revolution.

Back to the present reality: for the moment, you still need the distributor. Without that distributor, nobody sees your product, and the studios and the theater companies are going to run that. You can post your movie on the Internet, but currently, maybe one in *many* thousands might get a chance to direct a commercial after his or her digital movie is seen and discovered on the Internet. If you don't have big name actors, it's much harder to get people to tune in to you. And the people who control those big names are usually the agents and the studios. It's hard to predict how many years it'll take for that to change. For the person who has that spark, who can tell a story better than anybody else, film festivals are still the place to attract the people who pay money to show films. At the same time, the approach of shooting on your own camera, editing in your house on Final Cut Pro, and putting your movie on the Internet and the film festival circuit is getting young digital artists more exposure than ever before. New directors and writers can tell a story and show it to an audience in a few days — for a filmmaker, it doesn't get much better than that.

THE WRAP
If you had been talking to us at a Hollywood cocktail party, now would be the time that you'd ask us, "So what's my take-away from all this?"

The lessons we've come up with are:

1. The ease and accessibility of digital storytelling lures some people into shooting their movies before the script, crew, actors, or pre-production are ready. Don't cheat yourself by foregoing careful development, casting, or planning, or by thinking that it's easier and cheaper to fix things in post than to do them right the first time.

2. The best post-production is good pre-production. See above.

3. One of the best ways to make your money back on a digital project is to be cold-bloodedly realistic in planning for your target audience and taking care of annoying details like rights clearances.

4. The absolute best way to make your money back is to not spend so much on your movie in the first place.

5. If something makes money, the film industry will support it, whether it be a technology, a movie, or an individual talent.

6. Digital projection is still more expensive than, and doesn't look as good as, film projection, but the day will come when it makes sense economically and looks better than what you're seeing on film today.

7. The new digital projection standard will probably be 4000 instead of 2000 lines of resolution. As formats continue to evolve, this 4K standard will greatly increase the shelf life of digital content, since there's no technology that can tell you what used to be *between* the scan lines you've captured and up-rezzed. If the data isn't there, you can up-rez it all you want.

8. People have different agendas when discussing digital technology. Some people are looking out for their company's interests (stock value, turnaround time on projects, profit, reputation) when proclaiming the virtues of hardware, software, processes, or trends. Do your own research and make your own decisions.

9. The film industry is still very difficult to break into, get noticed in, and sustain success in. Digital image acquisition gives film-makers different tools and more access points, but the over-crowded and fickle nature of the marketplace remains the same.

10. The best reason to make digital movies is because you love the process, want to keep refining your craft, and are passionate about the story you have to tell.

11. If you have a story you want to tell, there is no excuse not to go out and tell it.

Digital technology has already proved that the democratization of filmmaking is not just talk. Take a movie like *The Fast Runner*, set in the Arctic and giving a marginalized community a way to reach the rest of the world with its voice and imagery and stories. *The Fast Runner* won the Camera D'Or, the highest achievement award for a first-time director, at the Cannes Film Festival. In fact, *Celebration*, *Dancer in the Dark* and *The Fast Runner* all won consecutive top prizes at Cannes. It didn't matter that they were shot in digital, just that the stories and the films were compelling.

Imagine video cameras in the hands of people in countries all over the world so that they all can tell their stories, so that there are no barriers to seeing stories from other countries, instead of seeing maybe one Iranian film per year, if you can get to an art house theater in New York or Los Angeles. Widespread access to digital cameras will help people realize that movies are not some magical thing that only other people can create. And that they can use images to communicate with anyone in the world, literally take ideas out of their heads and give someone else the means to share it. With video, there's something very fundamentally understandable anywhere in the world, because everybody is looking all the time.

It's like the invention of the printing press and the resulting spread of literacy and knowledge, but in an even simpler and more direct form. The image of a child playing, or people fighting, or lovers kissing is immediately understandable across cultures. Like those images etched into the Voyager space ship, they concretize the human need to share the stories of our experiences and imaginations and aspirations. Digital advances mean that the human interconnection has more evolution in store, and that's a hopeful thought.

# APPENDIX I
>>> **WHO'S LOOKING FOR DV PRODUCTIONS**

Many of the companies mentioned below have been profiled by this book, but they are by no means the only ones in their fields.

Capital Entertainment Group	*www.CEGgames.com*
300 Lenora Street #360	
Seattle, WA 98121	
(206) 405-4433	

Capital Entertainment Group seeks out game ideas for development, creation, and distribution

HD Net	*www.HD.net*
2909 Taylor Street	
Dallas, TX 75226	
(888) 919-HDTV	

Chairman, co-founder, and owner Mark Cuban is looking for high-definition product to broadcast on his three HD Net television channels, which currently feature sports, movies, and concerts. He is looking for completed product

Film Movement	*www.filmmovement.com*
10-14 Saddle River Road	
Fair Lawn, NJ 07410	

Film Movement buys the rights to art-house films that do well at festivals but have not gotten distribution elsewhere. The company then distributes the movies on DVD, selling them directly to audiences through a DVD-of-the-month club, in the same way that a book-of-the-month club lets its subscribing members keep the merchandise

Cinetic Media
(formerly known as Sloss Special Projects)
555 West 25th St., 4th Floor
New York, NY 10001
(212) 627-9898

www.cineticmedia.com
www.slosslaw.com

Cinetic Media specializes in producer representation (securing distribution for independent features and other content), providing consulting services to end users and media financiers worldwide, and securing financing for packaged motion picture projects

Open City Films / Blow Up Pictures
44 Hudson Street, 2nd Floor
New York, NY 10013
(212) 587-8800

www.blowuppictures.com

Profiled in Chapter 10

InDigEnt
135 West 26th Street, 5th Floor
New York, NY 10001
(212) 929-7711

www.indigent.net

Profiled in Chapter 10

Madstone Films
85 Fifth Avenue, 12th Floor
New York, NY 10003
(212) 989-4500

www.madstonefilms.com

Profiled in Chapter 10

Visionbox Media Group • Visionbox Pictures   *www.visionbox.com*
3272 Motor Avenue, 2nd Floor
Los Angeles, CA 90034
(310) 204-4686

Profiled in Chapter 10

Ifilm   *www.ifilm.com*

Easy to put your film on the site, but it's swamped with content

Atomfilms-Shockwave   *www.atomfilms.com*

Harder: AtomFilms seeks quality films and animations for worldwide commercial distribution to their network of television, airline, home entertainment, and new media outlets, including their award-winning AtomFilms Web site. They accept live-action and animation submissions with running times under 30 minutes.
Currently they are seeking the following content for specific distribution deals:
G/PG- 13 Animation, 10 minutes and under
G/PG- 13 Comedy, action and suspense, 15 minutes and under
G/PG- 13 Star Power, 15 minutes and under
PG/R Extreme, 3 minutes and under

American Film Market   *www.afma.com*

Annual congregation of thousands and buyers and sellers from all over the world

MIFED   *www.mifed.com*

The European counterpart to the AFM

| The Independent Feature Project (IFP) Market | *www.market.ifp.org* |

Formerly known as the IFFM

| Film Festivals | *www.filmfestivals.net* |

Worldwide links and information, as well as an online community of independent filmmakers

| Production Information | *www.productionhub.com* |

Industry Search, Marketplace and Community listings offer a nation-wide production directory of film, video, and digital media professionals, products, services, classifieds, event calendars, and news headlines

APPENDIX II
>>> SETTING UP YOUR OWN DIGITAL STUDIO

This appendix assumes you don't want to rent, and that you want a basic setup: not crazy high-end, but not the absolute cheapest thing either.*

Consult with cinematographers, editors, and do-it-yourselfers before making your purchasing decisions. The following Web sites may also be helpful:

Video Expert	*videoexpert.home.att.net*

Detailed technical articles comparing video formats and offering videography how-to

Tool Farm	*www.toolfarm.com*

Software and reviews

Price Grabber	*www.pricegrabber.com*

Comparison shopping on electronics, computers, and software

BASICS OF A DIGITAL STUDIO

Item	Specifics	Cost	Notes
Digital Videocamera	Panasonic AG-DVX 1000 24P Mini-DV	**$3500**	Keep in mind that this 24fps camera still has the limitations of 5-to-1 data compression and 4:1:1 capture (see chapter 4)
Tripod and head	Bogen – standard model	**$150**	However, you can spend up to $2000 on one of these if you want. You could also get a serviceable tripod for as little as $50.
Computer	Macintosh Power G4 with DVD-R/CD-RW drive	**$2700**	2MB processor; memory upgrades cost as much as you want to spend. This is the fastest Mac before their "ultimate" machine at $3800, which gets you more speed and memory. However, you might use that extra $1000 better elsewhere in setting up your own studio.
Computer monitor	17" CRT monitor, Mitsubishi Diamond Plus 74	**$200**	
Computer monitor (high-end)	20" Apple Cinema Display, flat panel	$1300	1680x1050 pixel resolution
Computer monitor (go crazy)	23" Apple Cinema HD, flat panel	$2000	1920x1280 pixel resolution
Final Cut Pro 3.0		**$900**	
TV monitor	Any 9"	**$250**	For playback
TV monitor (higher end)	LCD Digital 15"	$400	For playback
Approximate total of basic bolded items		**$7700**	Before sales tax, shipping, and extras such as power cables, connector cables, and additional accessories

OPTIONAL EXTRAS

Item	Specifics	Cost	Notes
AfterEffects 5.5	Standard package	$650	($1500 for Production Bundle with extra-groovy graphics tools)
Magic Bullet	(A plug-in to AfterEffects 5.5)	$995	Creates a filmic look *if* you don't intend to get your digital movie transferred to film
Cinema Tools	(For Final Cut Pro)	$900	Allows you to create an edit decision list for use with time coded footage

*We have not included professional microphones or sound recording equipment, which should be rented for use when shooting. If you record on a DAT, you'll need to keep access to a deck so that you can use the tapes in editing.

APPENDIX III
>>> RESOURCES FOR DIGITAL FILMMAKERS

The companies mentioned below have been profiled by this book, but are by no means the only ones in their fields.

UNION AGREEMENTS

Screen Actors Guild agreements with pay scales and basic contracts for different budget levels of production	*www.SAG.com*

> Standard agreement
> Low-budget (under $2 million)
> Modified low-budget (under $500,000)
> Experimental (under $75,000)
> Student film

If you are going to work with SAG actors, you must be aware of the union regulations and mandatory courtesies to which they are bound, accustomed, and entitled. It is much better to follow the rules (this includes using Screen Actors Guild extras), get the required signatures and permissions, and carefully document your trail, than to deal with a dispute after the fact or, worse yet, have your production shut down and fined for violations (ranging from payment issues to a failure to provide basic amenities like a private dressing area, restrooms, and drinkable water). Even if you don't intend to hire SAG actors, SAG rules offer a valuable reference guide for how actors (not to mention the rest of the crew) should be treated. Restrooms and drinking water may sound like no-brainers, but a lot of things go out the window in the heat and mania of production. Treating people well, being respectful of their needs and requests, and anticipating how to make them feel comfortable and taken care of, pays off tenfold in performance and morale.

Writers Guild of America agreements with pay scales and basic contracts for different budget levels of production, whether the writer is a Guild member or not	*www.WGA.com*

TO GET THE LOOK OF FILM ON VIDEO (Chapter 7)

Filmlook
2917 West Olive Ave.
Burbank, California 91505
(818) 845-9200

www.filmlook.com

Magic Bullet
5225 Wilshire Blvd.
Suite 705
Los Angeles, CA 90036
(323) 933-8262

www.theorphanage.com
Software available at
www.toolfarm.com

DIGITAL VIDEO-TO-FILM TRANSFERS (Chapter 8)

Cineric
630 Ninth Ave., Suite 508
New York, NY 10036
(212) 586-4822

www.cineric.com

Digital Film Group
James D. Tocher, President
316 East 1st Ave., 2nd Floor
Vancouver, BC V5T 1A9
(604) 879-5800

www.digitalfilmgroup.net

Heavy Light Digital
115 W. 27th, 12th Floor
New York, NY 10001
(212) 645-8216
(310) 821-1962 L.A.

www.heavylightdigital.com

DIGITAL VIDEO-TO-FILM TRANSFERS (Chapter 8) CONTINUED

Swiss Effects
Thurgauerstr. 40
CH-8050 Zurich
 41 1 307 10 10 Switzerland
(212) 727-3695 New York

www.swisseffects.ch

Tape House Digital Film
216 East 45th Street
New York, NY 10017
(212) 319-5084

www.tapehouse.com

RENTALS (Chapter 4)

World Wide Broadcast Services
Jeff Shapiro, Vice President
2111 Kenmere Avenue
Burbank, CA 91504
(818) 841-9901

ADVICE

Tutorials and articles about
all aspects of filmmaking,
both digital and analog

www.cyberfilmschool.com

Step-by-step guide to digital
video production and
Internet distribution

www.newvenue.com/flicktips

ADVICE *CONTINUED*

Extensive hands-on advice from a digital cinematographer	*www.geocities.com/victorfilmgroup /index.html*
Detailed technical articles comparing video formats and videography how-to	*videoexpert.home.att.net*
For those who want to make their own DVDs	*www.dvdrhelp.com*

OTHER RESOURCES

Absolute Character Tools: character animation software based on realistic, anatomically accurate muscle and skin movements. Plus a lot of really great demos to look at	*www.CGcharacter.com*
Their resource center lists companies in or supporting digital entertainment, media, and technology	*www.digitalcoast.org*
Everything you ever wanted to know about it	*digitaltelevision.com*
Portal for peer-to-peer sharing that so far has skirted piracy issues by simply providing the transport ability and not the content	*www.kazaa.com*

OTHER RESOURCES CONTINUED

Comes with audio CD	*Producing Great Sound for Digital Video* by Jay Rose
Industry Search, Marketplace, and Community listings offer a nationwide production directory of film, video, and digital media professionals, products, services, classifieds, event calendars, and news headlines	*productionhub.com*
High-end post-production pipeline and services	*www.showrunner.net*
On the self-distribution of issue-oriented independent movies	*Taking it to the Theaters* by Barbara Trent
Behind-the-scenes tutorial on compositing, showing how some of the amazing visuals and battle scenes were accomplished, plus an interactive exercise that lets you create your own Orc and composite your own scene	*www.lordoftherings.net /effects*

Michael Wiese Productions offers a comprehensive   *www.mwp.com*
catalog of books for filmmakers, writers, and
other media artists. Check out *Digital Moviemaking*
by cinematographer Scott Billups, *The Complete
Independent Movie Marketing Handbook* by indy
veteran Mark Bosko, and *Digital Filmmaking 101*
by guerrilla filmmakers John Gaspard and Dale Newton,
just for starters. Also visit MWP's online forum to
participate in ongoing advice sessions and creative debates

Print-on-demand DVD duplication   *www.CustomFlix.com*
for filmmakers who want an inexpensive
and efficient way to distribute their own films

Thorough, practical advice on how   *The Plot Thickens:*
to make your storytelling more effective   *8 Ways to Bring*
and compelling. Written by one of New York's   *Fiction to Life*
top literary agents   by Noah Lukeman

The stories behind the stories of   *The Big Deal:*
Hollywood screenplay sales, from the   *Hollywood's*
buyers' perspectives   *Million-Dollar Spec*
  Script Market
  by Thom Taylor

ONLINE PUBLICATIONS

www.filmandvideomagazine.com

www.digitalcinemamag.com

www.broadcastengineering.com

www.videosystems.com

www.theASC.com (American Cinematography)

MUSIC LICENSING AND DO-IT-YOURSELF SCORING

Music licensing fees are required for composers and performers. Even if you're using music in the public domain, any recording of that music (unless, say, you play it yourself) is also governed by licensing. For example, if your movie used a recording of Eric Clapton playing Mozart's Sonata in C, the underlying music would be in the public domain, but Clapton's performance would not be

www.ascap.com

www.bmi.com

www.sesac.com

TO GET MUSIC WITHOUT LICENSING FEES:

$35 for MP3 download of individual songs *www.uniquetracks.com*
$109 to buy a CD-ROM bundle that (royalty-free music)
includes an audio CD as well as music in
the form of computer files for use in
computer editing. Full-length themes and
variations on the theme so that it sounds
like you actually paid someone to score your movie.
Once you buy the music, you get to use it, period.

>>> *FILMOGRAPHY*

28 Days Later, 2002. Directed by Danny Boyle (shot on digital)

8 Mile, 2002. Directed by Curtis Hanson

Annie, 1982. Directed by John Huston

Bamboozled, 2000. Directed by Spike Lee (shot on digital)

Beauty and the Beast, 1991. Directed by Gary Trousdale

Bowling for Columbine, 2002. Directed by Michael Moore

Boxes, 2000. Directed by Rene Alberto Gil (shot on digital)

Breaking the Waves, 1996. Directed by Lars von Trier

Buena Vista Social Club, 1999. Directed by Wim Wenders (shot on digital)

Camera, 2000. Directed by Richard Martini (shot on digital)

Cats and Dogs, 2001. Directed by Lawrence Guterman

Celebration, 1998. Directed by Thomas Vinterberg (shot on digital)

Charlotte Sometimes, 2002. Directed by Eric Byler (shot on digital)

Chelsea Walls, 2002. Directed by Ethan Hawke (shot on digital)

Chuck and Buck, 2000. Directed by Miguel Arteta (shot on digital)

Collateral Damage, 2002. Directed by Andrew Davis

Coming Out: A Collection of Stories, 2002. Directed by J. C. Calciano (shot on digital)

Coronado, 2003. Directed by Claudio Fäh

Courage Under Fire, 1996. Directed by Edward Zwick

Dancer in the Dark, 2000. Directed by Lars von Trier (shot on digital)

The Date (short), 2003. Directed by Michael Mayer (shot on digital)

Dopamine, 2003. Directed by Mark Decena (shot on digital)

E.T.: The Extraterrestrial, 1982. Directed by Steven Spielberg

El Mariachi, 1992. Directed by Robert Rodriguez

Episode II: Attack of the Clones, 2002. Directed by George Lucas (shot on digital)

Erin Brockovich, 2000. Directed by Steven Soderbergh

Everything Put Together, 2000. Directed by Marc Forster (shot on digital)

Falling Like This, 2000. Directed by Dani Minnick (shot on digital)

Fight Club, 1999. Directed by David Fincher

Final Fantasy, 2001. Directed by Hironobu Sakaguchi

Full Frontal, 2002. Directed by Steven Soderbergh (shot on digital)

Gattaca, 1997. Directed by Andrew Niccol

Gods and Generals, 2003. Directed by Ronald F. Maxwell

Independence Day, 1996. Directed by Roland Emmerich

Iron Giant, 1999. Directed by Brad Bird

Jaws, 1975. Directed by Steven Spielberg

L.A. Confidential, 1997. Directed by Curtis Hanson

Life Is An Attitude, 2000. Directed by Steven Raack (shot on digital)

Lovely and Amazing, 2002. Directed by Nicole Holofcener (shot on digital)

Minority Report, 2002. Directed by Steven Spielberg

Monster's Ball, 2001. Directed by Marc Forster

Mr. Holland's Opus, 1995. Directed by Stephen Herek

My Big Fat Greek Wedding, 2002. Directed by Joel Zwick

Ocean's Eleven, 2001. Directed by Steven Soderbergh

Piñero, 2001. Directed by Leon Ichaso (shot on digital)

Rhinoceros Eyes, 2003. Directed by Aaron Woodley (shot on digital)

Series 7: The Contenders, 2001. Directed by Daniel Minahan (shot on digital)

sex, lies, and videotape, 1989. Directed by Steven Soderbergh

Smoke Signals, 1998. Directed by Chris Eyre

Star Trek: Nemesis, 2002. Directed by Stuart Baird

Star Wars, 1977. Directed by George Lucas

Superstar: The Karen Carpenter Story, 1987. Directed by Todd Haynes

Tadpole, 2002. Directed by Gary Winick (shot on digital)

Tape, 2001. Directed by Richard Linklater (shot on digital)

Teddy Bear's Picnic, 2002. Directed by Harry Shearer (shot on digital)

Terminator 3, 2003. Directed by Jonathan Mostow

The Anniversary Party, 2001. Directed by Alan Cumming and Jennifer Jason Leigh (shot on digital)

The Blair Witch Project, 1999. Directed by Daniel Myrick and Eduardo Sánchez

The Fast Runner (*Atanarjuat*), 2001. Directed by Zacharias Kunuk (shot on digital)

The Guys, 2002. Directed by Jim Simpson

The Hulk, 2003. Directed by Ang Lee

The Lord of the Rings: The Fellowship of the Ring, 2001. Directed by Peter Jackson

The Lord of the Rings: The Return of the King, 2003. Directed by Peter Jackson

The Lord of the Rings: The Two Towers, 2002. Directed by Peter Jackson

The Matrix, 1999. Directed by the Wachowski Brothers

The Mothman Prophecies, 2002. Directed by Mark Pellington

The Poor and the Hungry, 2000. Directed by Craig Brewer (shot on digital)

Time Code, 2000. Directed by Mike Figgis (shot on digital)

Tortilla Soup, 2001. Directed by María Ripoll (shot on digital)

Traffic, 2000. Directed by Steven Soderbergh

Treasure Planet, 2002. Directed by Ron Clements and John Musker

Wake, 2003. Directed by Roy Finch (shot on digital)

Washington Heights, 2003. Directed by Alfredo Rodriguez de Villa (shot on digital)

Yank Tanks, 2003. Directed by David Schendel (shot on digital)

ABOUT THE AUTHORS

>>> Thom Taylor authored *The Big Deal: Hollywood's Million-Dollar Spec Script Market* (William Morrow/Harper Collins, 1999), has written for such magazines as *Variety, Locations, Millimeter,* and other magazines, and also wrote the first article for *Movieline.* Thom majored in social science and economics at UC Berkeley, film and television production at the American Film Institute, and received an MBA from the University of Southern California. He has spoken about Hollywood on over 200 NBC radio affiliates, National Public Radio's *MarketPlace,* and as a repeat guest on numerous other radio shows. His commentaries on the film industry have been featured on CNNfn's "Business Unusual," CBS Marketwatch, STARZ cable television network, and in a variety of print venues. He has also organized and moderated over 50 seminars at non-profit arts centers.

>>> A native of Bangor, Maine, Melinda Hsu has contributed articles and short stories to *Film Threat, Jane,* and other magazines and fiction journals, and wrote and produced her one-woman show, *Seventeen Bananas* (shot and edited on mini-DV). Melinda has worked as a musical director for youth theater and as a story analyst for Dustin Hoffman/Punch Productions and numerous other producers, agents, and independent filmmakers. Several screenplays of her own have been optioned for production. Melinda graduated from Harvard with a degree in history, and got her masters in film from Columbia University. She participated in the Warner Bros. TV Drama Writers Workshop, and is currently a staff writer for a network television series. Melinda and Thom live in Los Angeles with their tri-color beagle, Barnaby.

>>> For more information, visit *www.bigdealnews.com*

DIGITAL MOVIEMAKING
2nd Edition
All the Skills, Techniques, and Moxie You'll Need to Turn Your Passion into a Career

Scott Billups

This book is geared to professional-minded people who have hopefully had prior experience in some aspect of production and who understand the fundamental difference between a hobby and a career. It's about how to be successful at making movies by taking an opportunity to experiment and demonstrating your abilities.

Scott Billups' goal is to kick your professionalism, your toolset, and your image quality up a notch so that you can compete in the real world of cinema. There are no simple solutions, secret tricks, instant remedies, or gizmos that will turn you into a moviemaker. In fact, the odds are against you. But Billups promises that by the time you've finished this book, your odds of success will have improved.

"If you are in or entering the new world of digital filmmaking and you want to know everything about everything... read this book by Scott Billups. You'll be sorry if you don't."

— David Lynch, Director

"An individualist in a town where conformity can be a Zen-like state of grace, Billups is not afraid to lock horns with mainstream studios as he seeks to invent 'the new Hollywood.'"

— Paula Parisi, *Wired Magazine*

Scott Billups is an award-winning director/producer who has produced, directed and written countless feature films, television programs, and commercials.

$26.95 | 300 Pages | Order # 107RLS | ISBN: 0-941188-80-9

DIGITAL FILMMAKING 101
An Essential Guide to Producing Low-Budget Movies

Dale Newton and John Gaspard

The Butch Cassidy and the Sundance Kid of do-it-yourself filmmaking are back! Filmmakers Dale Newton and John Gaspard, co-authors of the classic how-to independent filmmaking manual *Persistence of Vision*, have written a new handbook for the digital age. *Digital Filmmaking 101* is your all-bases-covered guide to producing and shooting your own digital video films. It covers both technical and creative advice, from keys to writing a good script, to casting and location-securing, to lighting and low-budget visual effects. Also includes detailed information about how to shoot with digital cameras and how to use this new technology to your full advantage.

As indie veterans who have produced and directed successful independent films, Gaspard and Newton are masters at achieving high-quality results for amazingly low production costs. They'll show you how to turn financial constraints into your creative advantage — and how to get the maximum mileage out of your production budget. You'll be amazed at the ways you can save money —and even get some things for free — without sacrificing any of your final product's quality.

"These guys don't seem to have missed a thing when it comes to how to make a digital movie for peanuts. It's a helpful and funny guide for beginners and professionals alike."

> — Jonathan Demme
> Academy Award-Winning Director
> *Silence of the Lambs*

Dale Newton and John Gaspard, who hail from Minneapolis, Minnesota, have produced three ultra-low-budget, feature-length movies and have lived to tell the tales.

$24.95 | 283 pages | Order # 17RLS | ISBN: 0-941188-33-7

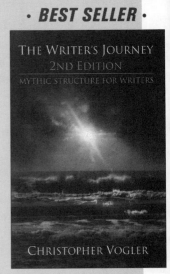

the Film director's
intuition
Script Analysis and Rehearsal Techniques

Judith Weston
Author of the best-selling book DIRECTING ACTORS

THE FILM DIRECTOR'S INTUITION:
Script Analysis and Rehearsal Techniques

Judith Weston

The craft of directing is well known to include shot composition and understanding of the technology. But directors need to know how to prepare so that their ideas achieve a level of intuitive truth. This means deep script analysis, until the characters' inner lives and private joys and problems are human and idiosyncratic, and as real to the director as his own. And it means reading the actors' impulses and feelings — including those that the actors themselves may not know they have.

A filmmaker's most precious assets — not just for directing actors, but for all the storytelling decisions — are his instincts, imagination, and intuition. Judith Weston gives away the secrets that can keep an imagination alive and free a director's intuition, so everyone on the set can function at full creativity.

Includes chapters on:
> Sources of Imagination
> Goals of Script Analysis
> Tools of the Storyteller
> The Lost Art of Rehearsal
> Director's Authority
> Sample script analysis of scenes from *sex, lies, and videotape*, *Clerks*, and *Tender Mercies*

"Judith's method is wonderful because it is practical. She has given me numerous tools to solve problems on the set and to earn the trust of actors. Her classes and her book are invaluable resources to any director."
— Lawrence Trilling, Director
Alias, Ed, Felicity

Judith Weston has taught Acting for Directors for over a decade throughout the US and Europe, and is the author of the best-selling book, *Directing Actors*.

$26.95 | 350 pages | Order # 111RLS | ISBN: 0-941188-78-7

24 HOURS | **1.800.833.5738** | **www.mwp.com**

ORDER FORM

TO ORDER THESE PRODUCTS, PLEASE CALL **24** HOURS - **7** DAYS A WEEK
CREDIT CARD ORDERS **1-800-833-5738** OR FAX YOUR ORDER **(818) 986-3408**
OR MAIL THIS ORDER FORM TO:

MICHAEL WIESE PRODUCTIONS
11288 VENTURA BLVD., # 621
STUDIO CITY, CA 91604
E-MAIL: MWPSALES@MWP.COM
WEB SITE: WWW.MWP.COM

WRITE OR FAX FOR A FREE CATALOG

PLEASE SEND ME THE FOLLOWING BOOKS:

TITLE	ORDER NUMBER (#RLS _____)	AMOUNT
_____		_____
_____		_____
_____		_____
_____		_____
_____		_____
	SHIPPING	_____
	CALIFORNIA TAX **(8.00%)**	_____
	TOTAL ENCLOSED	_____

SHIPPING:
ALL ORDERS MUST BE PREPAID, UPS GROUND SERVICE ONE ITEM - **$3.95**
EACH ADDITIONAL ITEM ADD **$2.00**
EXPRESS - **3** BUSINESS DAYS ADD **$12.00** PER ORDER
OVERSEAS
SURFACE - **$15.00** EACH ITEM   AIRMAIL - **$30.00** EACH ITEM

PLEASE MAKE CHECK OR MONEY ORDER PAYABLE TO:

MICHAEL WIESE PRODUCTIONS

(CHECK ONE) _____ MASTERCARD _____ VISA _____ AMEX

CREDIT CARD NUMBER _____

EXPIRATION DATE _____

CARDHOLDER'S NAME _____

CARDHOLDER'S SIGNATURE _____

SHIP TO:

NAME _____

ADDRESS _____

CITY _____ STATE _____ ZIP _____

COUNTRY _____ TELEPHONE _____

ORDER ONLINE FOR THE LOWEST PRICES

24 HOURS | 1.800.833.5738 | www.mwp.com